Editorial

AF194429

Kurdish Voices

On 9 January 2013, Fidan Dogan, Sakine Cansiz and Leyla Saylemez were murdered at the Kurdish Information Centre in Rue La Fayette, close to the Gare du Nord in Paris. These three women were activists in the Kurdish cause. Sakine Cansiz, aged 54, was a founder of the Kurdistan Workers' Party (PKK). Fidan Dogan, aged 31, worked at the Centre and also represented the Kurdish National Congress, based in Brussels. Leyla Saylemez, aged 24, also assisted in the work of the Centre. Their assassin, Ömer Güney, used a silencer to suppress the sound of his gunshots. He died in December 2016, shortly before he was due to come to trial, so all the evidence of the Turkish State's involvement in the murders was not presented in Court.

So it was that, five years after the event, Murat Polat, who found the three women, was able to testify in public 'for the first time' about what happened on that night in 2013. He was one of some 30 witnesses at the Permanent Peoples' Tribunal on Turkey and Kurds, which convened at the Bourse du Travail in Paris on 15-16 March 2018. Antoine Comte, the lawyer who had taken on the case, preceded Mr Polat in giving evidence.

In this issue of *The Spokesman*, we concentrate on events in Turkey itself, in Anatolia in the predominantly Kurdish cities of Cizre and Diyarbakir, in particular in its historic district of Sur. The Tribunal heard testimony about the murder of civilian men, women and children, confined in basements in Cizre to shelter from bombardment by Turkish forces. Some of them were burnt to death: 'chemical or incendiary weapons (flamethrowers) were used', according to Mehmet Tunc, speaking on television from Cizre on 5 February 2016. In Sur in Diyarbakir, buildings in UNESCO World Heritage sites were reduced to rubble as residents were driven away by Turkish authorities. We reproduce in facsimile selected sections of the briefing prepared for the Tribunal, plus the recommendations included in the Tribunal's Judgment presented at the European Parliament in Brussels on 24 May 2018 (see below).

In May 2018, President Erdogan of Turkey came on a state visit to the United Kingdom, meeting Queen Elizabeth at Buckingham Palace and Prime Minister Theresa May in Downing Street. While hands were being shaken in London, Turkey was increasing its grip on Afrin in northern

Syria. Families displaced from Eastern Ghouta, near Damascus, as the Syrian government regained control of that region, now occupy houses vacated by Kurdish families, who fled Afrin city when it came under Turkish attack by land and air earlier this year.

Such is the decline in the UK's international standing that Mrs May is anxious to cultivate relations with President Erdogan, notwithstanding his and Turkey's record of murder at home and abroad, as well as crimes against Kurdish civilians in Anatolia and now in Syria. For Turkey is now a NATO 'uncertainty', in the terms of the latest published US *Nuclear Posture Review*.

The global nuclear era enters a more dangerous phase, as the United States and Russia reveal some of their plans. We reprint relevant extracts from the revised US *Nuclear Posture Review* and from President Putin's speech in March, prior to his re-election. Once again, a race for nuclear advantage is under way, given added impetus by attempts to jettison the 1987 Intermediate Nuclear Forces Treaty, which outlaws a class of shorter-range nuclear weapons. But this is not a race between equals. The US hasn't neighbours next door who are enrolled in a hostile nuclear-armed alliance. Russia, although extensive in territory and rich in natural resources, has a comparatively small population and a lower level of economic development; hence, Putin's 'Great Breakthrough' proposals for his six-year presidential term, until 2024. Russian historians Roy and Zhores Medvedev offer some cautionary comparisons.

* * *

Recommendations

The Permanent Peoples' Tribunal was called to evaluate the events committed between June 1, 2015 and January 31, 2017 in many South-East Anatolian cities with majority Kurdish inhabitants, as well as other crimes committed in Turkey and abroad, starting in 2003, when Recep Tayipp Erdogan assumed the office of Prime Minister. The Tribunal has not been able to deal with events following and in particular the offensive launched in January 2018 by the Turkish armed forces against the Afrin enclave in Syria and the Kurdish region of Rojava. In view of these further developments and the events which took place during the session held in Paris on 15 and 16 March 2018, the Court made the following recommendations.

The Spokesman
Kurdish Voices
Edited by Tony Simpson
Published by Spokesman for the
Bertrand Russell Peace Foundation
Ken Coates: Editor 1970 to 2010

Spokesman 139   2018

Subscriptions
Institutions £40.00 (ex UK)
£33.00 (UK)
Individuals £20.00 (UK)
£25.00 (ex UK)

A CIP catalogue record
for this book is available
from the British Library

Published by the
Bertrand Russell Peace
Foundation Ltd.,
Russell House
Bulwell Lane
Nottingham NG6 0BT
England
Tel. 0115 9784504
email:
elfeuro@compuserve.com
www.spokesmanbooks.com
www.russfound.org

CONTENTS

FSC
Mixed Sources
Product group from well-managed
forests and other controlled sources

Cert no. SGS-COC-006541
www.fsc.org
© 1996 Forest Stewardship Council

Cover: Cizre

ISSN 1367 7748   ISBN 978 0 85124 8769

CIZRE

1. Turkey must immediately end all military operations carried out by its army in Syria and must withdraw its troops to within its national borders ...

2. Turkey is obliged to investigate and punish the responsible persons for war crimes, ascertained by the Permanent Peoples' Tribunal, committed in south eastern Anatolia during the period from 1 June 2015 to 31 January 2017 ...

3. Turkey must restore the rule of law, release still-detained magistrates and journalists, restore the rights of teachers and magistrates (judges and prosecutors) who have resigned from July 2016, restore freedom of press and information, end the state of emergency and fully implement the European Convention on Human Rights ...

4. Prior immediate proclamation of all military activity truce, Turkey must resume negotiations in good faith for a peaceful solution to the conflict — interrupted on October 30, 2014 — and complete them within a reasonable time frame ...

5. At the conclusion of the peace agreement an amnesty must be issued for the crimes committed by all parties during the conflict and all still-detained political prisoners must be released ...

In conclusion, the tragedy that disrupts the South East of Anatolia and is causing incalculable suffering to the Kurdish people is not the result of a destiny that cannot be avoided. It is the product of the errors, burdened by time, of an unthinking dogma of nationalism, which, in the past, provoked the Armenian genocide. The Turkish and Kurdish people can avoid this fate, transforming this policy totally and eliminating its origins. Where today the fatal rituals of hostility and denial are carried out, tomorrow could see a restoration and flourishing of justice, friendship and peace.

www.tribunal-turkey-kurds.org

Events in the city of Cizre

Cizre is a town in Şırnak Province in the Southeastern Anatolia Region of Turkey, on the border with Syria, just to the northwest of the Turkish-Syrian-Iraqi tripoint. It is populated by a majority of Kurds in addition to Assyrian/Syriac people, Arabs (and Armenians previous to the Armenian Genocide). Cizre is located in a valley, surrounded by hills and the population is almost 120.000 persons.

Barricades start to appear in Cizre at the end of 2014, in support and solidarity of the Kobane resistance against ISIS attacks. As said, the barricades were a form of protests but also an instrument to protect the peoples protests against police raids and repression.

The barricades were build by the "Patriotic Revolutionary Youth Movement" YDG-H (Yurtsever Devrimci Gençlik Hareket); as the name suggest, a youth organisation involved in the political struggle for the Kurdish issue.

Several sources mention that, as a result of the police forces' aggressive behaviour towards the citizens in Cudi[24] neighborhood (arbitrary raids and detentions), in which four people were killed, the local youth had dug trenches. Cizre's co-mayor and Ercan Demir, Chief of the Police in Cizre ("İlçe Emniyet Müdürü") negotiated and after a promise that no more arbitrary raids

---

[24] Cudi is a Cizre neighbourhood.

and detentions would take place, the machines of the municipality refilled the trenches. However, as soon as the barricaded streets were accessible again, the police forces entered the neighbourhoods again with armed vehicles and started randomly firing in the area. Many people were injured, and one boy named Umit Kurt (14) got killed on 6 January 2015.[25]

Police claimed that the boy was armed and that he was shooting at them, but ballistics investigation, conducted later, showed that the boy had not shot any gun while no traces of powder were found on his hands and no gun was found close to the boy's body.[26]

New negotiations between representatives of the population and the authorities started after these events. Hatip Dicle [27] addressed the people of Cizre, reading out a message of Abdullah Öcalan about the necessity to protect the peace process. Dicle stated that the youth should stick to the non-protest decision in order to secure the peace process, in spite of the recent events in Kobane and Cizre.[28]

All of this, including the growing tension in the region due to the war in Syria, contributed to creating a feeling of tension and fear amongst the population of the area.

In accordance with Provincial Administration Law no 5442 Article 11/C [29] [30], a first curfew has been declared in Cizre district by the governor of Şırnak on 4 September 2015 at 20.00. It lasted until 12 September 2015. The second curfew was imposed on 13-14 September 2015 and a third one on 14-15 November 2015. The longest and continuous curfew was implemented between **14 December 2015- 03 March 2016** and lasted for 79 days.[31]

---

[25] https://m.bianet.org/bianet/siyaset/161338-cizre-de-14-yasindaki-umit-kurt-polisin-actigi-ates-%20sonucu-oldu

[26] Newspaper T24: http://t24.com.tr/haber/cizrede-oldurulen-umit-kurtun-balistik-raporu-polisleri-yalanladi,294137

[27] Hatip Dicle is the co-president of the Democratic Society Congress (DTK- "Demoktratik Toplum Kongresi"). H e visited Öcalan as a part of the Imrali Delegation. During the peace process Hatip Dicle was one of the people negotiating with the Government.

[28] Newspaper article: http://www.hurriyet.com.tr/hatip-dicle-cizrelilere-ocalan-in-mesajini-iletti-27969349
Newspaper: http://diclehaber50.com/news/content/view/439761?page=3&key=f2b7fad2fc3f84654b937cd18d84 Video: https://www.youtube.com/watch?v=qVDb4impFs0

[29] "Article 11 of Act No. 5442 Law on Provincial Administration : A)The governor shall be the superior of all general and special law enforcement forces and organizations. He shall take necessary measures to prevent crimes from being committed, protect public order and security. For this purpose, he shall employ the general and special law enforcement forces of the State; the superiors and officers of such organizations shall be obliged to immediately execute the orders issued by the governor.
B) B) The governor shall secure the border and coasts of the country, and execute all affairs relating to border and coastal security according to the provisions in force.C) C) The governor shall have the duty, inter alias, to secure peace and security, personal immunity, safety of private property, public well-being and the authority of preventive law enforcement. The governor shall take necessary decisions and measures to this end. Provisions of Article 66 shall apply to those who do not comply with such decisions and measures."

[30] The Diyarbakir Bar association argues that this law is insufficient to infringe on a massive scale on rights guaranteed by the Turkish Constitution and international human rights instruments to which Turkey adhered.
https://www.diyarbakirbarosu.org.tr/filemanager/cizre%20raporu%20ingilizce%20(1).pdf

[31] In according with Cizre Field Report: http://en.tihv.org.tr/wp-content/uploads/2017/10/Cizre-Field-Report.pdf

Picture of Cizre
after the last
curfew, in
March 2016.

According to a report published by the Diyarbakir Bar Association Ahmet ADANUR (Cizre District Governor) stated that *"The need of operation has emerged in order to neutralize the armed groups and remove trenches and barricades. The curfew and the length of the curfew are determined by the Governor upon briefing from security offices. The length of the period could change according to observations and assessments."*[32]

Most reports regarding the first curfew gave a number of casualties of 21. However, a report dated 20.10.2015 and prepared by the Türkiye İnsan Hakları Derneği - Human Rights Association of Turkey (İHD), TİHV (Türkiye İnsan Hakları Vakfı – Human Rights Foundation of Turkey, Diyarbakır Tabip Odası - Diyarbakır Chamber of Physicians (DTO) and Pratisyen Hekimler Derneği - Association of General Practitioners (PHD) raised the figure to 22, including the death of Mülkiye Geçgel, who suffered a wound caused by firearms during the curfew.

After the first curfew in Cizre the Commissioner for Human Rights of the Council of Europe, expressed his concerns regarding the situation in Cizre, underlining how *"public life, including essential services such as healthcare, and means of communication had been severely disrupted, and that entry and exit from the city had been barred, amid reports of disproportionate use of force by security forces against civilians"* and *"called for access to be granted to independent observers, in particular, the national human rights structures in Turkey"*[33].

Between 4 September and 12 September 2015, according to the report drafted by Mr. Tahir ELÇİ (President of Diyarbakır Bar Assoc.) and published on 21st September 2015, *"all main roads which provide entrance and exit to Cizre including the roads which pass from Turkey to Iraq and the International Silk Road, were blocked by military barricades; barricades were covered with barbed wires and security officers took up their positions behind sandbags. In the first few days of the curfew, vehicles were allowed to pass partially and after control.*

---

[32] Curfew in Cizre A survey report of events:
https://www.diyarbakirbarosu.org.tr/filemanager/cizre%20raporu%20ingilizce%20(1).pdf
[33] Council of Europe: Commissioner for Human Rights, Memorandum on the Human Rights Implications of Anti-Terrorism Operations in South-Eastern Turkey, 2 December 2016, CommDH(2016)39, available at:
http://www.refworld.org/docid/58c68e9f4.html [accessed 17 February 2018]

The armoured military or police vehicles and tanks besieged all around the town including highways which provides entrance and exit to Cizre. Our committee has observed on their limited visit on 5 September 2015 that all the barrels of tanks and armoured vehicles which were located on high hills and all dominant points were aimed at the city. During the curfew, it was not possible to enter or exit the town.

From the 4 September to 12 September during the curfew, all networks of cell phone operators were cut on the instruction of the Governor of Şırnak. During this time all communication means connecting Cizre to the outside world had been cut with a very few exceptions."[34]

According to Amnesty International the "*operations by police and the military in these areas have been characterised by the abusive use of force, including firing heavy weaponry in residential neighbourhoods*"[35].

Amnesty International (while erroneously describing the operations as "law enforcement") underlines that: "*The operations appear to be conducted with the intention of killing – rather than arresting -- members of the YDG-H, ignoring the requirement that intentional lethal force only is used when strictly unavoidable to protect life. Evidence also points to the fact that security forces have been reckless in their use of firearms, using heavy weapons in built-up areas in a way that is likely to cause casualties to unarmed residents. In the course of on the ground research following an earlier curfew in Cizre from 4 – 12 September 2015, Amnesty International found evidence that several deaths may have been caused by snipers at locations far from where clashes were taking place. Among those killed were children, women and elderly people, who are very unlikely to have been involved in armed clashes. More recently reported deaths have also followed this same troubling pattern. Investigations into deaths have failed to show any sign of progress. International standards protecting the right to life require that **lethal force by law enforcement agents, and particularly their use of firearms, be limited to self-defence or defence of others against imminent threat of death or serious injury. Intentional lethal use of firearms may only be made when strictly unavoidable to protect life. (Principle 9, UN Basic Principles on the Use of Force and Firearms).** While it is difficult to paint an accurate picture of the scale of the violations in the areas under curfew, there is little doubt that the Turkish authorities are putting lives at risk by using lethal force excessively and recklessly. The Turkish authorities must rethink both the aims and the methods of their law enforcement operations*"[36].

On the 16th of September, two days after the end of the first curfew, **President Recep Tayyip Erdogan** said in a television interview: "*The state has taken the steps that had to be taken. The governors have the authority. If one is to go on the street, he is a terrorist. The operation has to be able to be conducted freely. If my citizens want serenity, they will have it. |...| The more steps we took, the more some people felt disturbed. Why was the terrorist organization in search of representatives? Let us have a place in this as well, they said. First, they entered*

[34] CURFEW IN CIZRE A SURVEY REPORT OF EVENTS:
https://www.diyarbakirbarosu.org.tr/filemanager/cizre%20raporu%20ingilizce%20(1).pdf
[35] Amnesty International, *Turkey: End abusive operations under indefinite curfews* , 21 January 2016, available at:
http://www.refworld.org/docid/56a07f7e4.html [accessed 16 February 2018]
[36] Amnesty International, Turkey: End abusive operations under indefinite curfews , 21 January 2016, available at:
http://www.refworld.org/docid/56a07f7e4.html [accessed 16 February 2018]

parliament independently, then as a group. Then what is this situation now? The terrorist manifestations that are taking place in several parts of our country are disturbing our people. We took precautions for this." And also " **Cizre was the clearest example of this**", concluding "There is a decision we took earlier about this parallel terrorist organization: to pave the road for operations against all legal and illegal organizations that are threatening our national security. Our government has made all the legal arrangements for this. This is being followed up in all fields and we have started getting positive outcomes already. If you noticed, they are all fleeing out of the country. If you didn't commit any crime, then why are you fleeing? Because they don't know what's playing in the background. Our justice and our police are continuing the fight against them."[37]

Human rights organisations referred to a recent internal circular of the military encouraging forces on the ground by stating they should not fear prosecution as the institution would back them anyways. This suggests the authorities not only are aware of the violations committed but are also ready to cover them. As such, human rights organisations pointed to a centralized, planned and fully deliberate policy implemented by the Ministries of Interior and Defense"[38] .

After the first curfew the situation in Cizre gradually became again more tense, since there was an escalation of tension and fear.

A gradually militarization of the city was going on since September, but only after the national election on the 1st of November there was a constant inflow of police and military forces in the area. The Human Rights Foundation of Turkey reported on government side the participation of "Police Anti-terror Combat Team, Police Special Forces, Gendarmerie Special Forces, Military Forces and Riot Police.' Also, there are some unofficial teams which are both by themselves and publicly defined as JİTEM, Esedullah, Hançer [Dagger] Teams etc...[39]".

In particular, in the middle of November a new wave of arrival in the city of tanks, panzer and other kinds of armed vehicles lining up on the top of the hills around Cizre city occured.

Local newspapers report that on the 16th of December Special units forces (military, police special forces and gendarmerie special forces - ten thousand strong) from Isparta, Bolu and Sivas had been sent to Cizre and Silopi for a major operation under command of two brigadiers of the Cakirsogut Gendarmerie brigade and the Silopi brigade. According to these sources, the military is also present and is leading the operation in coordination with the other forces.[40]

An Amnesty International report published on the 21th of January 2016 states that "The law enforcement and military operations conducted in areas under curfew has been characterised

[37] Article: http://t24.com.tr/haber/erdogan-bunlar-lafa-geldigi-zaman-saz-lafa-geldigi-zaman-caz,309896
[38] Euro-Mediterranean Human Rights Network (EMHRN), EuroMed Rights and FIDH High-level Solidarity Mission To Turkey, 20-24 January 2016 , 24 January 2016, available at: http://www.refworld.org/docid/56fcca9a4.html [accessed 17 February 2018]
[39] THIV report on Cizre: http://en.tihv.org.tr/recent-fact-sheet-on-curfews-in-turkey-between-the-dates-16-august-2015-5-february-2016/
[40] Newspaper: http://www.sozcu.com.tr/2015/gundem/iki-ilcede-dev-operasyon-1010848/
Newspaper: http://www.internethaber.com/dev-pkk-operasyonu-10-bin-kisilik-ekip-iste-ayrintilar-1495264h.htm

by the use of heavy weaponry and sniper fire by the police and army, putting the lives of trapped residents at risk", and in order to allow that, "*details provided by the Minister of the Interior to parliamentarians from the ruling AK Party during a 8-10 January retreat ... that a total of 6,182 soldiers and 7,889 police took part in the operations*"[41].

The premeditated and organised nature of the subsequent operations appears clearly from the fact that at the end of the first week of December, teachers (which represent the majority of government workers and 80 % of which come originally from Western Turkey) received an SMS calling them to participate in a training program that started on 14 December and which was to be conducted in their hometowns

> *"Our teachers can (are suggested to) follow these seminars in their hometowns.*
> *We demand our teachers to avoid the coach station and find alternative ways to exit the Town."*

Therefore, 1.298 teachers from Cizre and the surrounding villages, left the district.[42]

Few days later the longest and bloodiest curfew declared in Cizre started.

A document, dated **13 December 2015**, classified as *"secret"*, signed by the Prime Minister M. AHMET DAVUTOGLU gives instructions for the organisation of the curfew in the cities of Cizre and Silopi.

Below we produce the translation of the original document:

SECRET

TURKISH REPUBLIC PRIME MINISTRY

Directorate General for Security

Number:

Subject: Sirnak peace and freedom operation

Date: 13/12/2015

The state of the Republic of Turkey is carrying out operations effectively and resolutely, within the framework of the democratic rules of law, against the rural and urban structure of the separatist

---

[41] Amnesty International, *Turkey: End abusive operations under indefinite curfews* , 21 January 2016, available at: http://www.refworld.org/docid/56a07f7e4.html [accessed 16 February 2018];
- Human Rights Foundation of Turkey, http://en.tihv.org.tr/fact-sheet-on-declared-curfews-between-august-16th-2015-and-march-18th-2016-and-civilians-who-lost-their-lives/#_ftn1
[42] http://www.bbc.com/turkce/haberler/2015/12/151214_cizre_silopi

terror organization, that has been threatening the national security and the public order, targeting the security forces and the life and property security of the citizens. It has been confirmed by our security and intelligence units that the separatist terror organization "PKK", in particular using their urban structure, has;

- Been carrying out attacks that directly target the security forces and, in the first place, the right to life of our civilians, the right to freedom and security, the right of property and other fundamental rights and liberties alike,
- Been carrying out, by means of their armed forces, activities like blocking roads, verifying identities, racketeering and abduction, with the aim to impose a political and social pressure upon the region's people; and has not been permitting individuals, groups, communities, civil society organizations or political parties with different political, religious or world views to exist and forcing them to migrate, using systematic attacks,
- Been restraining our civilians from continuing their daily lives and profiting from fundamental civil services such as education and health, through acts like building mine and explosive loaded barricades and digging trenches, in the districts of Cizre and Silopi being in the first place, in our Province of Sirnak.

For these reasons, in order to establish a climate of peace in which our civilians will be able to exercise their fundamental rights and liberties, and the public order in a permanent way, in our Province of Sirnak, especially in the district centers of Cizre and Silopi, I request these requirements regarding;

1. The assignment of the Turkish Armed Forces with all of their means and capabilities for operational purposes, as a reference to the governors force request, within the framework of the provisions of the 5442 numbered Provincial Administration Law, in the districts of Cizre and Silopi and all other critical provinces/districts where it is deemed necessary,

2.The enforcement of the operations that will be executed in our province of Sirnak, within the command of the therefore dispatched senior commander of our military units, in the districts of Cizre and Sllopi in the first place, within the framework of the provisions of the 5442 numbered Provincial Administration Law, under responsibility and coordination of the Governor of Sirnak,

3. The usage of all components assigned for the operation (the Turkish Land Forces, the Special Forces, the Gendarmerie General Command, the General Directorate of Security and the Security Forces Command) according to the plan that will be made by the Operation Commander,

4. The announcement of a curfew by the Governor of Sirnak for the timeframe that is deemed necessary for the operations and the necessary precautions to be taken in order to provide the fundamental needs of our civilians, to provide the compulsory health services, to close off Ipek Road for as long as the operation requires and to secure a controlled traffic flow,

5. The reinforcement of the State Hospitals in Sirnak, Cizre and Silopi with specialists, medical staff and equipment for an uninterrupted twenty four hour service, by the Minister of Health, starting on 14th December; the assignment of ambulance planes and helicopters in Mardin Airport and the continuation of these precautions throughout the duration of the operation,

6. The temporarily closure of the schools in Cizre and Silopi by the Governor of Sirnak in coordination with the Ministry of Education, from the 14th December 2015 on,

7. The assignment of a sufficient amount of judges and prosecutors in the legal services of both districts, in order to assign one prosecutor on duty in all neighborhoods (nine neighborhoods in total), by the Ministry of Justice, from the 14th December 2015 on,

8. The precautions to be taken by The Ministry of Transport, Maritime Affairs and Transportation in order to ensure Mardin Airport and Serafettin Elçi Airport to continuously stay open throughout the duration of the operation,

9. The running of the operation centers assigned for the operation with the presence and cooperation of representatives of the National Intelligence Organization, the General Directorate of Security, the Gendarmerie General Command and the Prosecutors Office,

10. The waging of the procedures regarding the estimation and compensation of the damage in that might occur as a result of the operation, in the framework that applies, by the Governor of Sirnak,

11. The urgent provision of the Turkish Armed Forces, the Governor's Office, the Gendarmerie General Command and the General Directorate of Security with financial resources for all of their needs regarding this operation,

12. The assignment of experienced staff to the Governor's office of Sirnak, Cizre and Silopi, by the Ministry of Interior,

13. The conduct of press, public relation and strategic communication activities regarding the operation by, the Office of Public Relations Coordination, and therefore the assignment of more staff to the Governor's Office of Sirnak; and the support of the public organizations in this field, regarding strategic communication to be given to the Office of Public Relations,

14. Not allowing any actions to take place that would distance our citizens from the State and that could be subject of exploitation by the terrorist organization, during the operation and the application of the measures representing the State's authority; showing the affection of our State and making our citizens feel that the State is on their side, to be fulfilled.

Signed by AHMET DAVUTOGLU

LIST OF DIVISION

Order:

- General Staff of the Republic of Turkey

- National Intelligence Organization's Office

- Office of Public Relations

- Ministry of Justice

- Ministry of Interior

- (General Directorate of Security)

- (Gendarmerie General Command)

- (Governor's Office of Sirnak)

- Ministry of Finance

Information:

- Ministry of Defense

The document shows clearly the magnitude of the planned operation, the involvement of the Turkish Armed Forces leaving little doubt as to the fact that the operation goes far beyond a law enforcement action.

The curfew that started on 14 December 2015

The curfew was imposed on several neighbourhoods, in particular, Cudi, Nur, Sur and Yafes. But all the city was affected by this military operation.

The curfew was announced by a declaration of the Governor of Sirnak, Ali Ihsan Su[43]:

English translation:

Press release 14.12.2015

In accordance with the Article 11/C of Provincial Administration Law no 5442 a curfew is declared on 14.12.2015 at 23:00 in our Cizre and Silopi cities in order to counteract members of Separatist Terrorist Organizations, eliminate barricades and ditches trapped with mines and explosives by members of separatist terrorist organization and to provide security for life and property to our citizens and public order.

Separatist Terrorist Organizations have carried out attacks with mines, explosive-trapped barricades and trenches aimed at our citizens', fundamental rights and freedom such as the right to live, freedom, security and property. These acts have caused pecuniary and non pecuniary damages to our citizens, disrupted daily lives and hindered the access to basic public services and mainly health services.

---

[43] Report of THIV: http://en.tihv.org.tr/wp-content/uploads/2017/10/Cizre-Field-Report.pdf

In the district centers of Cizre and Silopi, with the intention of providing an atmosphere of peace and public order where our citizens can enjoy their fundamental rights and freedom, all kinds of moral and financial support will be provided to our citizens. In this sense, I ask my citizens to feel reassured and offer my sincerest love and respect to all of our citizens.

Respectfully announced to the public.
14.12.2015 Governor of Şırnak"

The day after the curfew was announced, the Prime Minister Ahmet Davutoğlu spoke to the press: *"Several of our districts have been cleansed of terror elements through successful operations. Inshallah, a secure environment will also be established in Cizre and Silopi. The operations there are only directed at the terror organisation"* [44]

On 13 or 14 December, as results from a recent commemorative declaration describing the birth of the group, the so-called "second phase of resistance to self-management" was started, through the establishment of the YPS.

According to the statement *"The aggressive and military-backed, war-principled way in which the resistance that was developed through our people's self-administrative organizations such as the neighbourhood councils, the communes and the YDG-H type youth movements were received, has caused the process to evolve completely into a military fight and war. In such an environment, the founding of the YPS by our people, which is their local self-defence body, has turned into a resistance epos that would last ten months in total, from its very beginning"* and underline that *"components of the military and the police were put in action, such as the Police Special Forces (PÖH), the Gendarmerie Special Forces (JÖH), the Bordeaux Helmets, the Blue Helmets etc. ... A strategy was used, using all these forces and methods of warfare, in which all areas of resistances were surrounded first and then targeted for annihilation."* [45]

On the 16 December, in a public speech, the Prime Minister Davatoglu declared *"The Special Operations Gendarmerie (JÖH) and Special Operations Police (PÖH) teams will work together. The operations will be carried out with air support. Addresses that were previously chosen by the intelligence services will be entered simultaneously. If necessary, troops from the land forces will also provide support"* stating that *"the button on the operation was pushed, to ensure 'unconditional' and 'literally' safety with 10,000 teams"* and then that *"If necessary house by house, street by street and neighbourhood by neighbourhood will be cleansed."* [46]

At the start of the operation the electricity supply in several districts of the city was cut i.a. by the destruction by state forces of local distribution cabins. The water distribution system was also cut. State forces fired also into water reservoirs placed on the roofs of the houses.

On 18 December, a serious water shortage was felt.

---

[44] http://www.imctv.com.tr/davutoglu-cizre-ve-silopiyi-ozgurluk-alani-haline-getirecegiz/
[45] Newspaper article: https://anfturkce.net/guncel/yps-unutmak-lhanettir-unutmayacagiz-100107
[46] Article: https://www.haberler.com/buyuk-operasyon-icin-dugmeye-basildi-7972536-haberi/

The same day, a public employee, İrfan Uysal was ordered to reopen the water central valve of the water distribution system. İrfan Uysal declared that this operation was organized with the knowledge of and after consultations with the police. While opening the valve he was shot by an armoured vehicle and was wounded, losing an arm[47].

At the same time, in parallel, the YDG-H, previously involved in demonstrations on the streets, started to organize themselves in order to protect the people from arbitrary attacks. The barricades and trenches, as mentioned above, were already present in the city. But due to theincrease in the militarization of the territory, in the middle of December, the YDG-H established the YPS as Civil Protection Units.

On December 20, the activities of the police showed a significant increase.

Targeting civilians

According to HRFT documentation centre, a constant number of civilian killings were recorded over the following days[48] resulting from a pattern of attacks by State forces. Güler Yamalak, 8 months pregnant, was shot in her belly by a sniper whilst trying to get her child to a doctor. She got dragged back into the house by family members. After long efforts and phone calls, they managed to get a permit to bring her to a hospital. She was saved but lost her child[49].

Civilians began to be targeted while doing their daily chores, even in neighbourhoods where there were no barricades, trenches or clashes.

Cahide Cikal, died after being hit by a shrapnel shell in her kitchen, in a neighbourhood (Kale Mahallesi) where previously and at the moment there were no conflicts.[50]

Several dossiers report similar events that took place in the following days.

A delegation of TIHV, IHD and SES reported that they "... *could make some observations and communicate with the people on the street.* According to this report it was clear that *"Families never came face to face with state security forces at the barricades. The barricades could be removed through dialogue. People were killed mostly by snipers and armoured vehicles that were deployed on the hills outside the city. ..."*

Some of the civilians that were killed in Cizre by snipers are:

-      Güler Yamalak, 20/12/2015 (pregnant, targeted on her belly, lost baby)

-      Miray Ince (baby Miray), 26/12/2015

-      Aziz Yural, 30/12/2016

-      Cabbar Taskin, 01/12/2016

-      Biseng Garan, 06/01/2016

---

[47] Cizre Report, pag. 63 e 64.
[48] CURFEWS IN TURKEY ACCORDING TO HRFT DOCUMENTATION CENTER (16.08.2015 - 22.03.2016)
[49] CIZRE 2ND CURFEW (December 2015-March 2016) HDP CIZRE REPORT (p. 35)
[50] CIZRE 2ND CURFEW (December 2015-March 2016) HDP CIZRE REPORT (p. 27)

- Veysi Elçi, 12/01/2016

- Mehmet Kaplan, 18/01/2016

According to the Human Rights Foundation of Turkey document "Curfews-Table-18-March-2016", the number of civilians killed in Cizre during the 79th days curfew, is 160 (34 children, 32 women, 14 people over the age 60). Besides, there are at least 59 bodies that were buried without waiting for the identification process.[51]

Access to health and medical treatment

A joint Euromed and FIDH mission reported regarding the sanitary situation and the access to health and medical treatment: *"the overall situation in areas affected by the armed conflict and the curfews is adverse to health: houses are in very poor conditions due to bombings, corpses are left in the streets and there is limited or no access to health facilities and personnel. The curfews and the fighting have heavily disrupted health services and made access to health very difficult for inhabitants of the concerned areas. Daily and routine care, for example to pregnant women and chronically ill persons (for example of diabetics), is highly disrupted or even impossible. The eviction or escape of hundreds of thousands of people also makes medical follow-up difficult and can have long-term effects on health (it is the case as children are not vaccinated, for example).*

The death of fighters and civilians in many cases directly results from limited or no access to health services. **Ambulances and medical staff are not allowed to enter zones under curfew.** *In some cases, doctors have mentioned that they managed to 'sneak in' on their personal capacity and rescue people, and to take ill or injured persons out to treat them. |...|* **To make the situation even more complex, human rights organisations reported that in many districts, security forces are using health facilities as their headquarters or barracks, and that armed forces sometimes fire from these buildings, making them de facto inaccessible to people in need of health assistance and endangering the lives of medical staff as well. In Cizre, 2 floors of the hospital are occupied by security forces, while the rest of the building is supposedly still working as a hospital, although the doctors' room was recently bombed. |...|**

The Human Rights Association of Şırnak reported that several injured young people from Cizre and Silopi were detained and brought to Şırnak for interrogation and prosecution. Several observers also reported that injured people were left to die on the streets, while persons trying to rescue them (medical personnel or citizens) were fired at or detained.

Indeed, as mentioned above, even interim measures ordered by the European Court of Human Rights regarding injured people were not applied and people died. **This is a clear violation of international humanitarian law and international human rights law.**

The State has an obligation to support and enable access to health to all without discrimination, and security forces as well as non-state fighters must guarantee that the

---

[51] XLS HRFT-Curfews-Table-18-March-2016.xlsx - TİHV

wounded are spared and medically treated whatever their status of wounded (combatants) or civilians. **Medical staff members are also victims of violence**, either as "collateral victims" or because they are directly targeted. Furthermore, one doctor was recently detained in Mardin and is now facing trial, while another 6 medical workers face judicial investigation for "propaganda of a terrorist organisation" for exercising their duties.

Medical staff that cares for the injured irrespective of their side in the conflict faces pressure and harassment from their hierarchy within the Ministry of Health. Professionals, as well as institutions (such as the Dicle University Hospital), have been subjected to smear campaigns depicting them as "supporters of terrorists" for treating injured fighters of PKK as well as governmental forces.[52]

Physicians for Human Rights (PHR) report: "Since *July 2015 numerous health care workers have been charged with the crimes of making terrorist propaganda and being part of an illegal organization. Those not formally charged have been subjected to administrative inquiries by the Ministry of Health for participating in protests calling for peace in the southeast, making statements to the media about the need for peace, and, in some cases, for providing medical treatment in areas under curfew to alleged members of armed opposition groups.*"[53]

Turkish authorities have charged health care workers using both provisions of the Turkish Penal Code and of the Law on Fighting Terrorism.

The Law on Fighting Terrorism defines selected provisions in the Turkish Penal Code as "terrorist offences" and prescribes specific criminal procedures for addressing them when committed on behalf of a terrorist organization, as defined by Article 1 of the Law on Fighting Terrorism.

Provisions often used include:
- *Article 220 of the Turkish Penal Code: "A person who makes propaganda through the medium of press and media about the goals of an organization which has been established in order to commit crimes" can be imprisoned for three to nine years;*
- *Article 7(2) of the Law on Fighting Terrorism: "Those who assist members of organizations constituted in the manner described above or make propaganda in connection with such organizations shall be punished with imprisonment of between one and five years."*
- *Article 7(1) of the Law on Fighting Terrorism includes Articles 313, 314, and 315, which include offences committed as part of an illegal organization, which are then criminalized under the Law on Fighting Terrorism when committed for an organization defined by Article 1 of the Law.*

---

[52] Euro-Mediterranean Human Rights Network (EMHRN), Turkey Human Rights under Curfew, Report of a *EuroMed Rights and FIDH High-level Solidarity Mission To Turkey, 20-24 January 2016*, 24 January 2016, p.7, available at: http://www.refworld.org/docid/56fcca9a4.html [accessed 22 February 2018]
[53] Southeastern Turkey: Health Care Under Siege "A hospital that was damaged by clashes during a 79-day curfew from December 14, 2015 to March 2, 2016 in the city of Cizre in southeastern Turkey".

The city was completely under siege and surrounded by security forces. Civilians were trapped in their houses. No efforts were made by the State to organise humanitarian corridors to evacuate the civilians.

On the 29th of December there was a huge explosion in the Nur neighbourhood and 3 police agents were killed. After this event, the situation became worse.

After two weeks of curfew, most of the upper floors of houses had been hit by shells[54] and snipers were posted on the roofs.

*"The attacks intensifying. Shelling continued in the town, as did the constant fire from armoured vehicles. **On 1 January 2016**, the 19th day of the curfew, those who thought the curfew would be of around two weeks duration, like the previous ones, left the neighbourhoods and went to the town centre, close to the municipality. Although talks were held with security officials regarding citizens who had been forced to leave their homes being put up in the Education Support Building, security officials told Cizre Co-Mayor Kadir Kunur that if citizens were placed there they would intervene harshly. A very small proportion of those who left the neighbourhood went to the Konak neighbourhood on the other side of the Tigris or to Şırnak city. **Three people were wounded after people were fired on as they left Cudi neighbourhood en masse. 6 people were also reported wounded in various ways.**"*[55]

While people remained trapped and were targeted even when they tried to leave the city or the neighbourhoods under siege, some decided to seek refuge and safety in the basement of the buildings.

Targeting civilians carrying white flags

On the **6th of January**, following a warning from the police to leave their house, the Garan family was targeted. 12-year-old Bişeng Garan was killed as the family tried to leave a basement carrying white flags with the knowledge of the police.[56]

This act clearly constitutes a war crime as defined in article 8 (2) (e) (i) of the Rome Statute:

"Other serious violations of the laws and customs applicable in armed conflicts not of an international character, within the established framework of international law, namely, any of the following acts:

(i)

Intentionally directing attacks against the civilian population as such or against individual civilians not taking direct part in hostilities;"

---

[54] Cizre Report (p.71)
[55] Cizre Report (p.75)
[56] Cizre Report (p. 77)

Subsequently the conflict in the city continued to deteriorate.

On **15 January**, government forces are able to force the barricades and enter the Nur district. But killing incidents continued to happen everywhere in the city; civilians continue to be targeted even in different neighbourhoods without clashes. In particular, from the data collected, it emerges that a large number of the killed, was hit in vital points of the body and reached by one or two shots of firearms, enough to be lethal.

On **20 January** a delegation (30-35 people) of civilians, journalists and local representatives, among whom Cizre Co-Mayor Kadir Kunur and MP Faysal Sariyildiz, are targeted in broad daylight whilst trying to help the wounded and recover of the bodies. After they had taken the bodies of Serhat Altun, Ahmet Tunç and Mehmet Kaplan and four wounded civilians, they left Cudi and headed towards Nusaybin Street (Cizre city centre). Although the delegation carried a white flag and was clearly identifiable as a humanitarian mission, the group was fired at by an armoured vehicle. This resulted in the deaths of two people and the wounding of **İMC TV reporter Refik Tekin.**

The local authorities had been informed and the delegation had been given the permit to move the bodies and wounded. In addition, a special application had been made to the ECHR, which had given an order of precaution on this specific request. So, MP Sariyildiz called the HDP group representative Idris Baluken, who on his turn contacted the minister of Interior Affairs but got ignored several times. Also, the governor decided to only respond via WhatsApp.

In this regards, HDP group representative Idris Baluken declared: "*We had made several phone calls with MP Sariyildiz. He had informed the* **authorities** *among whom the* **governor** *and had been told that they wouldn't experience any difficulties getting the bodies and wounded out of Cudi. Here in Ankara we had also informed the* **minister of Interior Affairs***. They gave them the permit and there wouldn't be any trouble they had said. After a parliament sitting that day, we went to see the minister personally and he there expressed his worries concerning this event. He said he would take care of it. We then got the news that the delegation still couldn't move. After not leaving the minister's office for another few hours, we heard that our friends had been taken to the municipality. In the meantime, two of them had died.*".

There is a video showing the attack conducted by an armoured vehicle on the group.

This constitutes clearly a war crime as defined in article 8 (2) (e) (i) of the Rome Statute cited above but also a the war crime of *"Intentionally directing attacks against personnel, installations, material, units or vehicles involved in a humanitarian assistance or peacekeeping mission in accordance with the Charter of the United Nations, as long as they are entitled to the protection given to civilians or civilian objects under the international law of armed conflict;"* as defined by article 8 (2) (e) (iii).

The attacks on basement shelters.

During this conflict, 3 series of incidents require a special attention. Due to the intensification of the armed conflict, people started to take refuge in basements.

Hereafter three attacks on basement were persons were seeking shelter from the violence will be further discussed in detail.

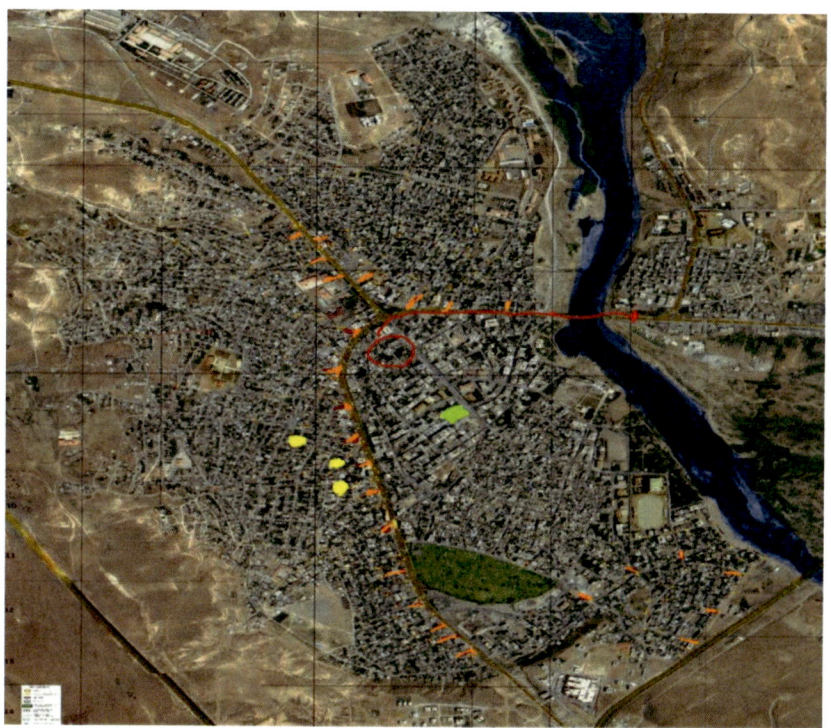

Legend: Yellow - basements   Orange - barricades   Green - Municipality

1st basement

On the 22 January the existence of the first basement became known.

The 1st Basement was located in Bostanci street n. 23, in Cudi neighbourhood under a 5-storey apartment block that was partially demolished after being hit by a mortar shell. This building was located 150 and 200 meters from the nearest barricades.

The HDP Şırnak MP Faysal Sarıyıldız was informed that from the 31 persons blocked inside the basement two had died and that many were wounded. He forwarded this information to the authorities and made it public through his twitter account.

From that moment on communications between the persons in the basement and the MP Faysal Sarıyıldız were organised daily.

On 25 January in the light of the detailed information received from those in the basement, the correct address had been shared with all the authorities, first and foremost the Cizre district governor.

On the same day Selami Yılmaz, one of the people hiding in the basement, died. Negotiations in Ankara between HDP MPs and Interior Minister Efkan Ala regarding ambulances being sent to the basement did not produce a result either.

Faysal Sarıyıldız reported on the meetings taking place in Ankara to DBP Assembly member Mehmet Yavuzel, who was one of those in the basement, in a short exchange of messages:

(Faysal Sarıyıldız)

13:49:27 Friend, they are not allowing a delegation. Our colleagues are still with the minister. We asked at least for them to stop firing.

13:51:14 A person who said that it was his house, called and said the address was 'Bostancı st, n.23"

13:51:32 We immediately forwarded this to our colleagues who are with the minister.
13:52:36 I'm sending your messages immediately.
13:52:46 I'm sending this one, too.

Mehmet Yavuzel

13:55:52 Aren't you coming to collect us in that delegation?
13:56:02 The apartment is being demolished over our heads.

In a continuing exchange of messages on the same day, Mehmet Yavuzel told Faysal Sarıyıldız that they were in a desperate situation and asked for a solution to be found immediately.

Mehmet Yavuzel

14:23:19 Let me say that for two days now some things are being said but now it is evening again and we haven't understood anything.... Tonight they could wipe us out. At least, the attitude to the building which we are in shows this clearly. You should know this.

If something concrete could be said to us as soon as possible. Let us at least know if we are to live or die.

(Faysal Sarıyıldız)
14:24:38 My friend, I am forwarding your message to the colleagues at the ministry and to our co-presidents.

Mehmet Yavuzel

14:29:24 No, there is no such thing … Let them come if we can come why should we insist. Do we really want deaths to occur? At least if a few of you could come and take us one by one… N. B: They have begun to shell us again…

(Faysal Sarıyıldız)
14:13:28 The minister rang the governor while our colleagues were with him, saying: "if that building collapses there will be trouble. Don't let it happen." Nothing is clear as to what the method will be. But if it continues like this and we don't get a result by this evening, I will set out with the mothers tomorrow. The colleagues say: 'if we don't get a result here, definitely do not go out," but at 09:30 tomorrow morning I will definitely come.
14:14:10 Is the building still being fired on?

Mehmet Tunç

14:19:51 A mortar hitting the chimney really scared us. Anyway, it exploded on the third floor, and all the dust from the stoves came into the basement. They are shelling the house.
14:20:56 And very badly.

After two hours:

Mehmet Tunç

16:51:51 Very bad and they are getting closer.
16:52:27 It doesn't seem like the world has heard the voice of Cizre, but what is there left to do for me? What can I do if I've upset some friends? I'm not well. There is a seriously wounded girl here, called Soltan. She is constantly "saying don't leave me, dad" and it's killing me. There is a thirteen-year-old boy who keeps asking for water, but we can't give him water as he has internal bleeding. Our heart is with you, comrade, I can't go downstairs, so tomorrow it should definitely be done.

(Faysal Sarıyıldız)
16:55:17 Be careful, don't go outside. We will not be part of this crime against humanity. We will definitely set out with the mothers tomorrow.

On 26 January HDP MP Faysal Sarıyıldız again tried to reach the place where the basement was situated along with a group of 15 family members of people known to be in the basement. They were stopped by the security forces in front of the Cizre Municipal building.

The same day Faysal Sariyildiz is informed by the people in the basement that the building is constantly being hit and the 2nd and 3rd floors are damaged very badly. The ceiling is said to no longer hold.

At the same time, in a public speech President Erdogan said to the governors: *"When you deem necessary, put aside the situation and act with your own mentality."* He hereby reassures that no one will be held responsible for their actions, no consequences.[57]

On 27 January HDP Group chair İdris Baluken, HDP Adana MP Meral Danış Beştaş and HDP Urfa MP Osman Baydemir met the Interior Ministry. As a result of the HDP members' efforts, permission was granted for the wounded to be collected from the basement. Following the meetings in Ankara, Şırnak MP Faysal Sarıyıldız met the district governor of Cizre and sought guarantees that ambulances could go to the basement to collect the wounded.

However, a short time later it appeared that instead of ambulances, armoured vehicles had gone to the area where the building was situated, that armoured vehicles stopped the ambulances and that health teams had been taken to the Police HQ in Konak neighbourhood. When the ambulances approached the area where the basements were situated, shots were fired from the armoured vehicles to give the impression there were clashes.

This situation was to continue in the following days.

The Şırnak governor's office issued a written statement in the evening regarding the 24 wounded. In the statement, it was said that: *"as a result of the organisation's barricades with booby trap bombs, trenches and their armed attacks on our ambulances and health teams our ambulances were unable to reach the address in question.*

Our ambulances were brought to the closest possible place and, if there were injured, they were asked to be brought to this point, but despite all our efforts, a positive response was not forthcoming from the injured and the callers."

---

[57] Cizre Report Turkiye (p.249)

On **27 January** Cizre People's Assembly co-chair Mehmet Tunç was connected to Med Nuçe Television, making the following statement regarding ambulances:

"The situation is really critical. They are intervening in the house. Let me inform colleagues of what will happen next. At the moment we have 5 corpses alongside us. People are facing execution or extermination. The situation is critical. At the moment I am upstairs. The sound of gunfire can be heard....The ambulance didn't reach us.
They are firing at the building from armoured vehicles. The door has been torn down. Everything is visible. The entire street can be seen.

The situation is really critical.... Speak to Faysal. It's as if they are inside the building. ... Our security of life is not important. From now on these people have no security of life left. Whatever will happen, let it happen.

If I go down they will probably firebomb. At the moment I'm on the second floor.... You can't hear anything except the sound of gunfire.. ...We have just exchanged messages with our friends.

They said: 4 municipal employees have set out to reach you. But just at the time they are about to leave it seems as if they are trying to finish the job with execution or a plot. So we connected to you and we said let's inform you of the latest situation.

This is the situation. Panzer 104 is visible. From the door I see an armoured vehicle is only ten metres away and it has completely demolished the door."

Baki GÜL (Med Nuçe Speaker): Can you see the ambulance?

Mehmet TUNÇ:

No, we've never seen an ambulance... We should at least get those who are alive out of here and leave the wounded. If the colleagues approve it we can leave this house. But while leaving there is the possibility of being shot by snipers. So we will either wait to be executed in the basement or leave the house and become targets of snipers. So colleagues, we must make a decision now. ...either we go to the basement and await execution, or we leave the building, at least 5 or 6 friends are okay, I mean they can get up. If we leave even if 1 or 2 people are shot dead at least 3-4 will have a chance of survival. I don't know the situation of the governor, or the district governor. But at the moment the forces here are firing at the house with the intention of destroying it."

Cizre People's Assembly co-chair Mehmet Tunç also made this appeal to public opinion in Europe and Turkey in a phone call to the 12th International Kurdish Conference being held on the same day in the **European Parliament on 27 January 2016**:

English translation:

"...The fine for breaking the curfew is 100 TL, but we go out and they give us a death sentence.

They are firing mortars. In Cizre they are using heavy artillery, mortars, everything.

A great massacre is taking place in Cizre and we are facing a huge genocide. All the houses have been bombarded. Tanks are being used. The AKP government and the Republic of Turkey are using weapons, which are supposed to be used against the enemy, against its own people in the 21st century. A tragedy is taking place in Cizre.

For 60 days the people have been hungry and thirsty.

Only ten thousand people are left out of a population of 120,000. The people have been forced to leave. Such policies were also used in the 1990s. 4 thousand villages were emptied and the people settled in districts like Cizre.

They emptied the villages saying the PKK would be finished off.

But now they say they will empty cities and finish off the PKK. I call on our friends in the European Parliament. A real tragedy is taking place in Cizre. 28 people were wounded in one house. Four of the wounded died. Of the 24, Nusret Bayar (she died soon after the phone call), Veli Çiçek and Sultan Irmak are graves. All the water has gone. We go out to get water and we are hit by snipers. We can't go out. The four-storey building has been demolished by mortars. In order to get a connection, I am in that demolished building. And the situation is critical. For this reason, we say to our friends there. Please stop this savagery. You have the power to stop this massacre in Cizre. You have the power to warn the AKP government and lift the blockade on Cizre. Otherwise, in the event of a massacre taking place, we will see you as an accomplice..." .

On **28 January** the ambulances were despatched 4 times, but permission was not given by the security forces for the ambulances to access the site, claiming a clash was taking place.

Minister of Health Muezzinoglu declared *"We have ambulances waiting around the corner. If they would have been honest they would have taken the wounded out and brought them to the ambulances, who are placed only 500 m away. But they're not honest, it's propaganda they're trying to make over the so-called wounded.[58]"*

In the same day, then Prime Minister Davutoğlu made the following statement regarding the basements in Cizre: *"Since the subject has come to the notice of our Interior Ministry our ministers and myself have followed it. All efforts have been made for our ambulances to access the scene of the incident. Everyone must be sincere. We are engaged in combatting terror, but whoever is wounded we will take all measures to get them to hospital. First, we'll treat them then we'll try them. No one can claim that while fighting terrorism in Turkey extra-judicial acts have taken place. If the injured in question are to be reached, which we want, then first of all*

---

[58] http://aa.com.tr/tr/saglik/saglik-bakani-muezzinoglundan-cizre-aciklamasi/511727?amp=1

terror centres must make sincere calls for them to surrender. We are monitoring developments, wherever there is a wounded person efforts will be made to reach them.[59]"

Contrary to these claims of Prime Minister Ahmet Davutoğlu, on **28.01.2016** DBP party assembly member Mehmet Yavuzel was connected by phone to the Med Nuçe Television channel, saying that for 6 days the authorities had strung them along by saying "*we are sending ambulances, which cannot get there because of clashes*", and misleading the public.

Mehmet Yavuzel said the following regarding what they were going through in the basement, and the situation of the wounded:

"*...At this moment there are 19 wounded. 5 of them are in a serious condition. The others are unable to walk. There are also 6 dead bodies, people who've been murdered. Some of the people here are KJA activists, some are DEM-GENÇ, there are university students, civilians. For 5 days I know ambulances have been coming.*
They say they'll take us, I don't know what else. Every time they send the ambulances back, saying there's a clash. So we have understood this: the fact that they send the ambulances, then prevent them getting here, shows they have different intentions. At least that is the conclusion that emerges.
Now today the Constitutional Court has taken another decision: 'there may be armed people amongst them, military people'. As they are so interested they should come and look. We are already surrounded. Next to and behind the building there are armoured vehicles. They're playing janissary music.
We can hear them 24 hours a day. Reconnaissance flights come over. Then they say these things, which are solely designed to deceive the Turkish people and public. Public opinion should know this. For 5 days the same things, the same lies are being uttered. For 2 days people here have had no liquids. People will die because of this. They should be aware of this.
Our people who are waiting outside Cizre should know this. Our people in Cizre should know this. Our people living in Europe should know this. There are 6 civilian corpses next to me. And 19 wounded, they cannot get any liquids. They are all on top of each other. Has there ever been such a scene in human history?
The area of this building is being bombed every day. Three floors have collapsed. Every time a bomb falls the place fills with dust and people here cannot breathe. Today a youth has probably died from thirst and cold during the bombing. (As he speaks the groans of the wounded can be heard).
Ferhat Karaduman is gravely ill and may die at any moment. Sultan Irmak, Serhat Saltıkalp, Mustafa Gazyak. They may also die at any time. As I said they have had no liquid for 2 days. They say: 'safe area'. 'Bring them to a safe area'.
People cannot go 20 metres to get water. People who can hardly walk cannot go and get water. The building is being bombed from all sides. 20, 50 times a day. People are tired of explaining the situation. We can no longer find anything to say.

---

[59] https://www.birgun.net/haber-detay/davutoglu-ndan-havalimaninda-cizre-aciklamasi-ambulanslarin-olay-yerine-ulastirilmasi-icin-calismalar-yapiliyor-102132.html

> *All public opinion should know that what has gone on for the last 6 days has been a delaying tactic. That is, by doing this they want the people here to die. Or they want the security forces to finish the job. If they are delaying it means they have different plans.*
> *So public opinion and our people should know this. Our people waiting outside Cizre, all the educated people in the whole of Kurdistan, young people, women, likewise our people in Europe should know.*
> *These people have not had liquid for 2 days. If this goes on for 2 more days, even if they are healthy they will die. And no one will be able to explain, so our people should come to the neighbourhoods of Cizre without worry, recognising no obstacle. They should come and take their children."*

On the **29th January** President Erdogan, answering a question from journalists, declare: *"They're lying that no ambulances were sent. The ambulances were there, maybe there were just no wounded."*[60]

In the same day, from the basement they send a message in which was written *'we have a phone with a camera, but we don't use it because when it is switched on the battery runs out. We will try and if we can send them we will.'* Then they used a normal phone, one which had a long lasting battery, to send the names of 25 people who were still alive. 16 of them wounded and 9 uninjured but exhausted. According to this, the names of the people trapped in the **1st Basement**, are: Mehmet Yavuzel, Rohat Aktaş, Feride Yıldız, Ferhat Saltıkalp, Ali Fırat Kalkan, Mustafa Vartiyak, Mustafa Aslan, Tahir Çiçek, Rıdvan Ekinci, Dersim Aksay, İslam Balıkesir, Serdar Pişkin, Ferhat Karaduman, Sultan Irmak, Sercan Uğur and Fehmi Dinç were wounded, while Hacer Aslan, Gülistan Üstün, Sakine Şiray, Berjin Demirkaya, Ramazan İşçi, Mahmut Duymak, Kasım Yana, Osman Gökhan and İzzet Gündüz were worn out from hunger and thirst.

On **29 January** those in the basement told to MP Faysal Sarıyıldız that the security forces had got quite close to the building, that their shoes were visible and their conversations had been heard.

On **30 January**, after receiving guarantees from the **Crisis and Coordination Desk** established by coordination of the Prime Ministry, Interior Ministry and Health Ministry, the health teams and ambulances waiting at the Cizre municipality set out for the basement at around 09.30.

Ambulances from the Health Ministry were accompanied the municipal ambulances. The ambulances and health teams went to within 150 – 200 metres of the basements and waited for approval from the **Crisis and Coordination Desk**. From the desk the HDP delegation was told that if the wounded emerged from the basement within 15 minutes, approval would be sent for their collection. The delegation maintained constant telephone contact with the wounded in the basement while awaiting approval. After a delay of about half an hour, while

---

[60] Cizre Report Turkiye (p.112)

waiting for approval from the **Crisis and Coordination Desk** a loud explosion and the sound of gunfire was heard from the basement, which were heard over the telephone. The screams of the wounded were heard, and they said: *"They are firing at us, a bomb has been thrown in, they're going to kill us. Help, what do they say."* These moments were recorded.

A dialogue that took place between DBP PM member Mehmet Yavuzel, who was wounded and later died in the raid, and Meral Danış Beştaş while the ambulance was moving and at the moment of the raid: (This dialogue was also listened into simultaneously by government officials by means of tele-conferencing.)

First transcription

Meral Danış Beştaş: At the moment we are monitoring the ambulance. It's on the way.
Mehmet Yavuzel: Yes.
Meral Danış Beştaş: Let it arrive, then we will call you.
Mehmet Yavuzel: Okay. It's quiet here....
Meral Danış Beştaş: Okay, okay. I will call you once the ambulance arrives.
Mehmet Yavuzel: Just so you know, it's quiet here.

Second transcription

Meral Danış Beştaş: We've just spoken to the ministry. Everyone will be on the phone.
Mehmet Yavuzel: Yes.
Meral Danış Beştaş: Get prepared. They have just given approval, but...
Mehmet Yavuzel: Okay.
Meral Danış Beştaş: When we call you, you will go out.

Third transcription

Meral Danış Beştaş: Have the noises stopped? The sound of the police.
Mehmet Yavuzel: Ha, they're here, in the corridor.
Meral Danış Beştaş: They are in front of the door from which you will exit.
Mehmet Yavuzel: Yes, they're inside.
Meral Danış Beştaş: They're inside.
Mehmet Yavuzel: Maybe they can hear your voice. The phone is on. Is the Interior Minister with you?
Meral Danış Beştaş: At the moment that telephone...(Just at that moment there is the sound of an explosion, gunfire and screams from those in the basement)

Fourth transcription

Meral Danış Beştaş: Hello
  Mehmet Yavuzel: My ears are bad, I can't hear.
Meral Danış Beştaş: Your ears are bad. Can you hear me?
  Mehmet Yavuzel: Very little.
Meral Danış Beştaş: Very little. I'm shouting at the moment, shouting. If you're not in a position to leave we'll have to find another formula.
  Mehmet Yavuzel: We're under rubble. How can I explain!
Meral Danış Beştaş: Okay, okay, so you're not in a position to get out.
  Mehmet Yavuzel: we're under the rubble, rubble!
Meral Danış Beştaş: Okay, okay, keep the telephone on. They can't leave, they can't get out.

Despite government officials saying the necessary humanitarian interventions would be made immediately, no positive development occurred while there was telephone contact between the wounded and the delegation. Following the attack, only two telephone conversations took place at intervals. During these calls the wounded said they were under rubble, that they were having difficulty breathing, that they were unable to move and would be unable to leave the building without support. Those stranded in the first basement said another person had died during the telephone conversation.

Following this conversation, the telephone connection was entirely broken.

Along with these developments, in telephone conversations made by the HDP delegation with the Prime Ministry, Interior Ministry and Crisis and Coordination Centre it was stated that the situation was of the utmost seriousness, that there were grave concerns regarding all the wounded and that those who were unable to move had to be taken from the building by health teams. Despite insisting for hours, they were informed by the Crisis and Coordination Centre that a rescue or health team would not be able to go there and that it would not be permitted. After a time, the HDP delegation's demand for two municipal employees and health workers to verify the truth of this information on the ground and administer first aid to the wounded was rejected by government officials, but after persistent talks with the Interior Ministry the demand was granted and two officers from the Cizre municipality and two health workers set off to reach the basement. However, this attempt failed on account of increasing gunfire and explosions. When the Health Ministry and Cizre district governor said it was not possible to guarantee the safety of these people, this attempt did not produce a result. While saying that since the officials could not ask the security forces to cease firing, such a thing was impossible, they said the municipal and health personnel would only be able to pass through the line of fire. As the firing continued, both the 112 ambulance, and the Cizre municipal ambulance and the health personnel had to withdraw around 3 pm.

On **31 January** a ten-person women's delegation consisting of relatives of those in the basement headed towards the basement carrying white flags with the intention of rescuing the wounded and of retrieving dead bodies. Those who approached the building were detained.

On the **2 February** a statement was made by the **Yekîneyên Parastina Sivîl - Civil Defence Units (YPS)**, which was involved in clashes with the security forces in Cizre, to the effect that they did not have any forces in the area where the basement was situated and that no clash had occurred there[61].

In according with the pre-investigation report on Cizre, made by Sebnem Korur Financi on the 3rd March 2016, *"When arriving at the first basement, an object likely to be a tank bullet was noticed on the window sill. |...| On the left-hand side, many burned bones and bone particles were found next to the wall. Amidst these particles, a piece was recognized to be mandible. When the length of the eyeglasses (belonging to an adult), as seen on the photograph, were compared to the measurements of the mandible, taking into account the loss of size as a result of a fire, it had to be accepted that the mandible was still not proportionate with the frame, thus did not belong to an adult but to a child around the ages of 10-12.[62]"*

According to statements by Human Rights Watch *"The evidence suggests, however, that the basements were fully surrounded by the security forces at the time the alleged killings took place. Furthermore, the authorities have given no compelling explanation as to why it was not possible in these circumstances to detain individuals alive or to evacuate allegedly injured people and civilians who were among those sheltering in the basements. The government has not claimed that those sheltering in the basements violently resisted while being evacuated.*

The picture of what happened after the alleged killings is also incomplete. Municipal workers told Human Rights Watch that they transported the bodies to the morgue in body bags after the military and police ordered them to collect the bodies from streets near the buildings where the three basements were located.

The municipal workers also said some of the bodies were burned, in some cases so charred as to be unrecognizable, and that others were missing limbs and heads. An imam who saw some of the bodies gave a similar account. Human Rights Watch also saw eight of the autopsy reports on the recovered bodies, which indicated that six bodies lacked body parts and four were burned. The autopsy reports note that such findings could be consistent with an explosion though did not explain why some were partially "carbonized", and in three cases determined people had been shot dead.

The Istanbul Forensic Medical Institute is conducting DNA testing to establish the identity of the dead. "[63]

The report further states that on **January 28,** *Human Rights Watch executive director, Kenneth Roth, met with a senior government minister in Ankara and reminded the Turkish government*

---

[61]Article:http://diclehaber50.com/news/content/view/497454?page=4&key=c4f60ee8111bf32c1b270ddb2b9e977c?page=1&key=c4f60ee8111bf32c1b270ddb2b9e977c

[62] Forensic Dossier: https://tihv.org.tr/wp-content/uploads/2016/03/3-Mart-2016-Cizre-%c3%b6n-rapor.pdf

[63] https://www.hrw.org/news/2016/07/11/turkey-state-blocks-probes-southeast-killings

about its obligation to permit injured people access to medical treatment, regardless of their identity, and asked for detailed information on whether the basement was surrounded by security forces and if the area was entirely under their control. The minister did not answer Roth's question but claimed that those in the basements were providing "contradictory information." He did not explain what he meant by this. The minister also said those in the basements did not want the ambulances provided by the state and were seeking to escape from the basements without being caught.

Pictures of wounded and death sent by persons in the basement

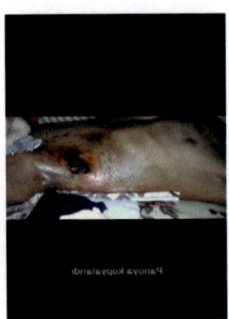
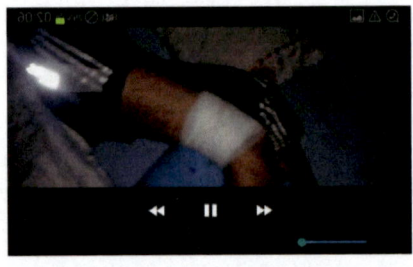

Pictures taken after the attacks on the basements

<u>2nd Basement</u>

A few days later, on the **4th February,** information was made available through the television channel Özgür Gün TV, that sixty-two people, most of them wounded, were forced to take refuge in the basement of a building located in Narin Street n. 6, always in Cudi neighbourhood, close to the 1st basement.

Amongst those in the basement was Mehmet Tunç who had escaped from the attack on the first basement later taking refuge in the second basement 150-200 metres away[64] Tunc called on telephone the TV channel to unveil the existence of the second basement. Mehmet Tunç explained what occurred in the following way:

---

[64] Cizre People's Assembly co-chair Mehmet Tunç had called the Kurdish Conference held at the European Parliament on 27 January, explaining what was happening in the first basement and making an appeal for international awareness. Since the area was entirely isolated and blockaded and communications were limited, although it is not certain what happened, most probably Mehmet Tunç left the first basement on the evening of 27 January or on 28 January and took refuge in the second basement. Mehmet Tunç died in that basement.

"...As a fire broke out on the second floor and mortars and tank shells had made holes in the building, all the old furniture and sofas and possessions from the house are in the basement, we are facing a Madımak Hotel incident.
This is a shame for humanity. ...
And this smoke has completely filled the building and the fire has begun to slowly come in through the holes. Although I'm trying to wet the sofas a great fire is coming down from above.
I know that at this moment there are fires everywhere in Cizre.
If we look from the Alize Künefe or the other side of the Nusaybin road, everyone who looks from three sides will see this fire. For that reason, I am calling on all humanity.
At least, rather than ambulances, the fire brigade should come and put out the fire. Otherwise there are people here without feet, gravely wounded people and children who will be burnt. I have no doubt that this will go down in history as Turkey's, as the whole of humanity's, even the United Nations' shame. ....
The householder left 17 demijohns of water downstairs, presumably for a day. In the last four days we have finished 5 or 6 of them. I have given them to the friends and they have finished them.

They are wounded people, they drink water. I have poured some on the radiators to dampen them, but upstairs is ablaze ... The fire broke out because of grenade launchers, tanks and mortar shells ... If only we had a video cell phone so that you and the whole world could see these sights, the house which is ablaze".

On **5 February** Mehmet Tunç was connected to Med Nuçe television, saying incendiary weapons were being used against the second basement.

He said:

"Here conventional or incendiary weapons are being used. Last night we used four or five demijohns of water to prevent the whole house being burnt, but 9 people lost their lives. Şervan Adıgüzel, Ercan Pişkin, Muhammed Öztürk, Nizar Isırgan, Cengiz Samsak, Ramazan Çendek and others we don't know, their faces were completely burnt. I am underlining this: when tomorrow or another day these bodies are found the AKP government will endeavour to bury them quickly because they know what they have done is shameful.

Chemical or incendiary weapons (flamethrowers) were used.

The house turned into a fireball. My hand and face are burnt. The faces of those who died have puffed up. When we removed their clothes we saw they were charred. I couldn't touch those who died, who were slaughtered. Those who were wounded have puffed, swollen faces and I am as sure as I am of my name that banned weapons were used.

I, therefore, call on the United Nations, to existing humanity, to say that there must be an examination made. They must examine what weapons these people were killed by. I don't think it was by fire. The fire was small. It's true that it reached the house, but as we were putting it out inside it suddenly turned into a fireball. This was a weapon and we saw people burning.

In my bag I had nearly 100 doctor's masks, just in case. These masks have gone black, with a flammable smell. Perhaps they will intervene now. These dead, murdered people should definitely not be buried by their families.

The United Nations should analyse them to see what banned weapons did this to these poor people. There are 13 and 14-year-olds in the basements. It's as if there are armed people there and they are burning and destroying the basements. They are just burning the basements and destroying them, but people are dying! … I spoke to İdris Baluken too.
The fourth floor has collapsed, these people here could all die. At the moment there are 28- 29 wounded and 9 corpses. Ekrem Söğülgen, Mehmet Aslan and the faces of 14 year old children have been burnt. Savaş Balcan, Fidan, Felek Çağdavul young student girls of 13-14. Yasemin Çakmak.

They are all middle school graduates.

Arin Pişkin, as I count them there are close to 28, some of them are unable to say their names because their faces are entirely burnt. Our fear is that with an intervention with a different weapon, with pepper gas, that these people will be slaughtered. I have been saying this for 60 days.

It is not too late, these people can be saved. Perhaps it is true, there are at the moment hundreds of people under rubble in Cizre. Maybe there are dozens of basements like this. This is just the tip of the iceberg. By chance, we came to this basement. These people are involved in a race against death. There are people in a really serious condition. They have suffered burns and there is no way to treat them …"

It was stated that the police, who surrounded the building with armoured vehicles, made constant calls on the wounded to surrender, saying those who complied would be taken to hospital by ambulance. 16-year-old Abdullah Gün[65] went outside to look for an ambulance but was shot dead. Since his body could not be identified for 15 days, correspondence was sent by the Silopi Public Prosecutor's office to the District Governor's office for it to be buried in a common grave.

On **6 February** the Şırnak Governor's office made a statement regarding the second basement, claiming: "Terrorists *who fled the building set it alight.*"[66]

On **7 February** Cizre People's Assembly co-chair Mehmet Tunç spoke by telephone for the last time on Med Nuçe Television, explaining the savagery what had happened in the second

---

[65] « Cizre HDP Report" (p. 120)
[66] Article: http://www.bbc.com/turkce/haberler/2016/02/160204_cizre_dokuz_kisi_olum_aciklamalar

basement, replying to the allegation made by the Şırnak Governor's office regarding the building being set alight by people who fled:

> "At the moment there are 51 people in this basement and I estimate that there are dozens of such basements in Cudi, Nur and Sur neighbourhoods. Some are wounded, some have serious burns. If these people are not treated their faces and hands will be detached. We applied emollient cream last night but this morning we saw that the cream had stuck to people's faces ... When we listen to FM radio they say people set themselves alight. So we need an urgent delegation of doctors and lawyers to come to Cizre to examine the wounded and the dead. Although we tried to keep the dead bodies in the basement, due to the smell we have had to put them outside.
> We know that tomorrow or in the future guns will be placed next to the bodies and they will tell the press: 'they were terrorists, members of an armed organisation,' but these people were killed in the basement by flame throwers.
>
> Wounded friends are still with us.
>
> No one should be buried before they are examined, because for days we have seen the AKP burying these bodies hurriedly in order to portray itself as in the right to the UN and the world. Our people are also remaining silent, therefore from now on no bodies should be buried in Cizre."

The same day, on the **7 of February**, there was a **huge explosion** in the city, heard by all the people living in the area.

TRT's news item concerning the 60 people 'rendered ineffective' was denied the next day by then Prime Minister, Ahmet Davutoğlu. The HDP's constantly asked question regarding the whereabouts of the remaining people which remained without answer.

Between 9th and 10th of February, the number of corpses brought to the Cizre state hospital was thirty nine. On 11 February thirty-one more bodies were brought to the Cizre state hospital.[67]

After the end of the curfew, the place where was located the building was completely destroyed and parts of bodies were found by citizens in the rubble and on the banks of the Tigris river.

> Events in a third basement are also documented in the Briefing prepared for the Tribunal. For reasons of space, this section is omitted.

---

[67] Cizre Report (p.122)

Events in the district of Sur in Diyarbakir city

Sur is the name given to the old city of Diyarbakir within the old city walls. The first settlement in the area is dated 5000 BC and since Diyarbakir has been a very important meeting point at the intersection of East and West. It is a multilingual, multi-cultural and multi-layered city.

There were 569 registered historical buildings in Sur. Many of these were destroyed in the conflict as explained hereafter.

Sur consists of 15 neighbourhoods and in 2015 had a total population of 50.341. [76]

Forced displacement[77]

In Surici totally five times curfews have been declared by the governor between beginning in September 2015 and lasting several days. Particularly the six neighbourhoods Cevat Paşa, Dabanoğlu, Fatih Paşa, Hasırlı, Cemal Yılmaz ve Savaş have been affected by these 24-hour blockades through the security forces. The last curfew dating on December 11, 2015 is valid for five neighbourhoods. Armed skirmishes, curfew and blockades set up by special police forces and the gendarmerie, continued in five neighbourhoods, and were extended to the neighbourhoods of Ziya Gökalp, Süleyman Nazif, Abdaldede, Lalebey and Alipasha from 27 January 2016 to 03 February 2016. The Diyarbakir governor's office declared on the 10 March 2016 that operations had come to an end.

During these curfews similar attacks as those described above on the population of Cizre occurred in Sur.

Hereafter however the emphasis will be on a different type of problem: the chain of successive and complementary actions by the authorities that have led to the forced displacement of more than 20.000 inhabitants of Sur.

The successive steps that have led to this result were:

- The systematic destruction of buildings, including historical buildings, houses, mosques etc. by artillery bombardments during the clashes in Sur with Kurdish militants in the period of 9 September 2015 to 10 March 2016
- The decision taken by the Council of Ministers on 21 March 2016 to expropriate 6292 out of 7714 parcels in Sur.

---

[76] Nevin Soyukaya, Archaeologist, Former head of the UNESCO World Heritage Site "DIYARBAKIR FORTRESS AND HEVSEL GARDENS CULTURAL LANDSCAPE", DAMAGE ASSESSMENT REPORT, Conflict Period and following Demolition of the Old city (SURİÇİ) of DIYARBAKIR, August 1, 2017

[77] Unless otherwise indicated all data in this part are drawn from Nevin Soyukaya, Archaeologist, Former head of the UNESCO World Heritage Site "DIYARBAKIR FORTRESS AND HEVSEL GARDENS CULTURAL LANDSCAPE", DAMAGE ASSESSMENT REPORT, Conflict Period and following Demolition of the Old city (SURİÇİ) of DIYARBAKIR, August 1, 201

- The continued destruction of buildings under the pretext of cleaning the area of debris after March 10, 2016 leading to the total demolition of several districts turning large parts of the old city into flatlands.
- The modification of the Urban Conservation Plan by the Ministry of Environment and Urbanization in December 2016 paving the road for speculative so-called urban renewal plans that denature and distort completely the city and in particular its historical center.

The systematic destruction of buildings, including historical buildings, houses, mosques etc. by artillery bombardments during the clashes in Sur with Kurdish militants in the period of 9 September 2015 to 10 March 2016

Tanks were positioned around the districts of Sur in which curfews were declared. Initially the State Forces attempted to break through the barricades and trenches in one point, not far from the area where many historical monuments such as the Armenian Church are situated.

This lead to heavy fighting in which State Forces opposed heavy weapons, mainly artillery mounted on tanks, to mainly light weapons in the hands of a limited number of Kurdish fighters. These clashes resulted in considerable destruction in that area.

On 10 December 2015 the curfew was lifted for a limited number of hours. As a result of this that thousands of inhabitants of the districts under curfew left their houses and became refugees in their own town. The authorities took no measures to provide food, shelter, medical assistance etc. to these refugees. This resulted in the almost complete depopulation of this part of the city. Nevertheless a limited number of civilians did not leave their houses for various reasons.

After a few hours the curfew was re-established and witnesses report that from that moment on the systematic shelling of houses everywhere in Sur by artillery mounted on tanks started. According to the witnesses houses were shelled story by story, including in areas where there were no or very limited clashes on the barricades.

That systematic destruction process continued later, after the fighting stopped. Sattelite images from 10 May 2016, shortly after the end of the fighting, show that 10 hectares of buildings were completely destroyed (this will double later as seen hereafter to 20 hectares).

The decision taken by the Council of Ministers on 21 March 2016 to expropriate 6292 out of 7714 parcels in Sur.

After the end of state operations, on 21 March 2016 the Council of Ministers took a decision on the expropriation of 6292 out of 7714 parcels in Suriçi based on the article 27 of the law on expropriation. By this decision, 82% of the parcels in Suriçi shall be expropriated by the Turkish government. A large part of the remaining 18% is in the possession of the Housing Development Administration TOKI and the Treasury, i.e. of the Turkish state. As a result, Suriçi will be entirely passed into public ownership. This also means that the residents of these five affected neighborhoods will not be able to return.

Map of the area to be expropriated. Red indicates the parcels marked for expropriation. Blue parcels were previously already in the hands of the State:

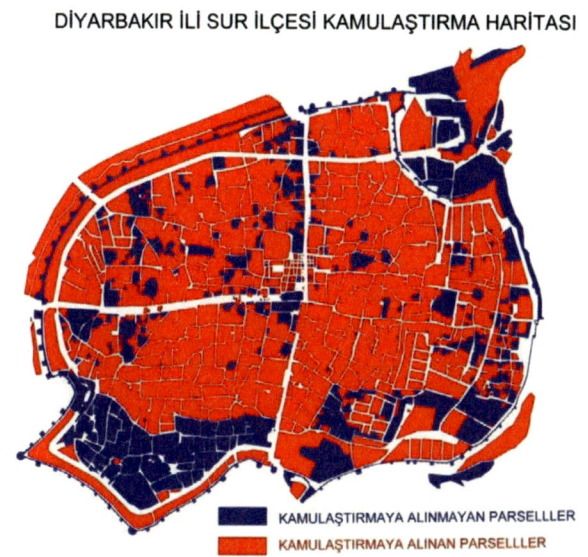

DİYARBAKIR İLİ SUR İLÇESİ KAMULAŞTIRMA HARİTASI

KAMULAŞTIRMAYA ALINMAYAN PARSELLLER
KAMULAŞTIRMAYA ALINAN PARSELLLER

The continued destruction of buildings under the pretext of cleaning the area of debris after March 10, 2016 leading to the total demolition of several districts turning large parts of the old city into flatlands.

Under the pretext of cleaning up the rubble and creating roads necessary for security reasons the authorities continued the destruction of several districts in a period of more than 1 year after the end of the fighting.

This evolution is clearly illustrated by the following images:

On 10 May 10 ha are completely destroyed.

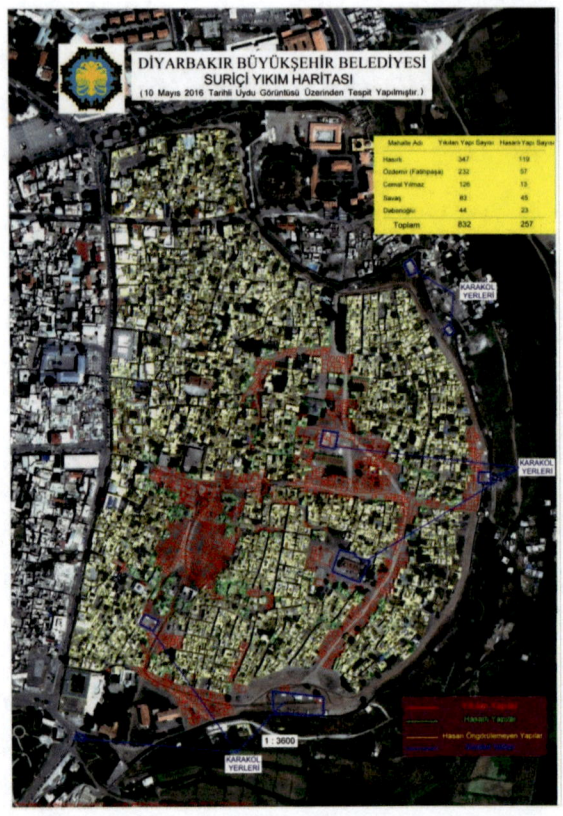

From the satellite image of August 16, 2016 below it has been assessed that a total of 1519 buildings and other constructions have been destroyed completely, among them registered civil and monumental buildings. The destruction covers 20 ha (double of the surface destroyed at the end on 10 May 2016.

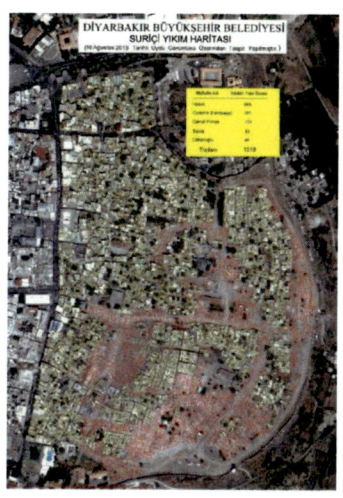

Picture taken from a commercial flight on 4 April 2017

Inside the walled city 19 April 2017

Picture taken from a commercial flight 4 May 2017 showing ongoing destruction

The modification of the Urban Conservation Plan by the Ministry of Environment and Urbanization in December 2016 paving the road for speculative so-called urban renewal plans that denature and distort completely the city and in particular its historical center.

Urban Conservation plans have subsequently been modified. The Diyarbakir branch of the Chambers of Architects and Engineers of Turkey has examined those plans and found 17 different violations of urban and conservation norms. The most important conclusion is that all the changes introduced are all justified on grounds of security and thus planning is reduced to an instrument of defence. The new houses that are built in the area are inaccessible to the original population of the destroyed districts.

The sequence of events and decisions of the Turkish authorities resulted in the forced displacement of 20.000 to 50.000 people from Sur. This amounts to a form of collective punishment of these persons for their supposed participation in § or sympathy for what started as an action of civil disobedience against the termination of the peace process by the Turkish State and the continued violation of the right of the Kurds to self-determination.

This constitutes:

- **a grave breach of the Geneva Conventions of 12 August 1949, namely the war crime of causing extensive destruction and appropriation of property, not justified by military necessity and carried out unlawfully and wantonly as defined in art. 8 2 (A) (iv) of the Rome Statute**
- **as well as the war crime of unlawful deportation or transfer as defined in art. 8 2 (A) (vii) of the Rome Statute**
- **as well as the war crime of Ordering the displacement of the civilian population for reasons related to the conflict, unless the security of the civilians involved or imperative military reasons so demand as defined in art. 8 2 (e) (vii) of the Rome Statute**
- **as well as the war crime of destroying or seizing the property of an adversary unless such destruction or seizure be imperatively demanded by the necessities of the conflict as defined in art. 8 2 (e) (xii) of the Rome Statute;**

Destruction of world heritage

Suriçi district as a whole, was registered as "Diyarbakir Urban Archeological Site" in 1988. Since the first master plan to protect this area could not be implemented, a new draft of the master plan was prepared and put into action in 2012. Following adoption of the new master plan, Diyarbakir Metropolitan Municipality started to work for recognition of Diyarbakir Fortress and Hevsel Gardens as world heritage by the UNESCO as of 2012. In parallel to this, a "Site Management Plan" and conveyed to World Heritage Center in August 2014. During the 39th meeting that took place in 4th of July, 2014, World Heritage Center approved Diyarbakir Fortress and Hevsel Gardens as a cultural landscape that is the world heritage. Diyarbakir Fortress, İçkale, Anzele Water Body and Hevsel Gardens are considered as the heritage zone while Sur and Tigris Valley area were registered as the buffer area.

The Sur buffer area is since then protected by international laws as well as by the Turkish Cultural and Natural Heritage Protection Act no. 2863. These international agreements signed by Turkey: UNESCO Universal Declaration on Cultural Diversity (2001), The Convention for the Safeguarding of Intangible Cultural Heritage (Paris, 2003), Convention Concerning the Protection of the World Cultural and Natural Heritage (Paris, 1972), Convention for the Protection of Cultural Property in the Event of Armed Conflict (The Hague, 1954), Venice Charter (1964) and The Declaration of Amsterdam (1975).

A report drafted by the Diyarbakir Metropolitan Municipality[78] reports e.g. the following damages to historical buildings:

- Kurşunlu Mosque, which is a registered intangible cultural heritage located in Fatihpaşa neighbourhood, suffered irrevocable damage at its northern front walls as well as its' stoop pillars located within the mosque. A fire destroyed the sanctuary and created distortions in walls, decorations and ornaments were destroyed as a result of the fire. Moreover, the fountain of the mosque that was reconstructed is now totally destroyed (Photos 1 & 2).

COURTYARD OF KURŞUNLU MOSQUE

---

[78] Diyarbakir Metropolitan municipality, "Cultural heritage Damage Assessment report on Sur, Diyarbakir, 30 March 2016, p. 4-5

- Sheikh Muhattar Mosque, that is quite well-known with its Minaret on the Four-Pillars was equally damaged. Two of four carrier pillars of the minaret were targeted by heavy weaponry and carrier lintels of the minaret were also damaged.

The MINARET ON FOUR PILLARS (ON THE LEFT)

Moreover, visual evidence also shows that walls of the mosque were partially destroyed to facilitate entrance of armoured vehicles into the street.

- With the same pretext, registered historical shops were destroyed which are located at Yeni Kapı Street which adjoin the biggest Armenian church in the Middle East, Saint Giragos and Chaldean Church next to it and thus the historical texture of the street was also destroyed too.

The Yenikapı street, with an original width of 8m before the demolition, has been turned into a 15 m wide street.

- One of 7 public baths/hamams in Suriçi which could survive up until today, Pasha Hamam, was damaged in the early days of armed clashes. Afterwards the cooling section of the hamam was totally destroyed as a result of a fire outbreak.

- Another registered historical building, an example of traditional civil architecture, turned into Mehmed Uzun Museum House by Diyarbakir Metropolitan Municipality was partially destroyed. Amongst the part destructed, there is also kabaltı (street veil) section, which represents one of rare examples of traditional street texture of Diyarbakır which enabling pedestrians to walk under the physical structure. Furthermore, it is also detected that a series of other historical civil architecture examples were partially or totally destructed. As a result of devastations, the area characterised as "Urban Archeological Site" has lost its' unique street and physical structure fabric in a way that cannot be restored.

Other destructions are reported by Nevin Soyukaya, Archaeologist [79]:

- Aerial photographs underline that the Hasırlı Mosque, located at parcel no. 235/19 has been completely destroyed and the debris removed, without a trace left in its place.

- **Armenian Catholic Church:** The bell tower, south courtyard wall and pool in the courtyard have been destroyed completely and the main entrance door and church outbuilding located to the west of the church have been destroyed partly. Also a wide road through the area has been opened.

---

[79] Nevin Soyukaya, Archaeologist, Former head of the UNESCO World Heritage Site "DIYARBAKIR FORTRESS AND HEVSEL GARDENS CULTURAL LANDSCAPE", DAMAGE ASSESSMENT REPORT, Conflict Period and following Demolition of the Old city (SURİÇİ) of DIYARBAKIR, August 1, 2017

After restoration in 2014

March 2016

May 2016

Nevin Soyukaya, Archaeologist, Former head of the UNESCO World Heritage Site reports[80]:

"The Diyarbakir governor's office declared on the 10 March 2016 that operations had come to an end. The governor of Diyarbakir declared the end of the operations in the affected area on March 10, 2016. But before the completion of the operations in February 2016 heavy equipment and bulldozers of state institutions have started with demolition in the area under curfew and the excavation of debris. A part of the debris has been dumped at a site of the Diyarbakir Dicle University and afterwards it has been covered with soil. This illegal action has been documented by the Environment Conversation Department of the Diyarbakir Metropolitan Municipality on February 29, 2016. In an area registered as urban conservation site and buffer zone of a World Heritage Site demolition and excavation of debris have been executed without assessing the state of the operations and clashes, without obtaining permission from the responsible Diyarbakir Region Conservation Board of Cultural Assets. The necessary permissions for the removal of the excavation were taken out only about a month later. The Conservation Board of Cultural Assets has stated in its decision with the no. 3873, dated 23 March 2016, that "the removal of debris obstructing streetways may be allowed under the supervision of the experts of the museum directorate; if debris from partially or completely destroyed registered buildings is encountered, then all significant construction elements should be kept at the original site in a proper way, under the supervision of the museum experts, for later assessment. An aerial photograph taken and handed by a citizen on April 4, 2016, and two satellite images commissioned by the Diyarbakir Metropolitan Municipality on May 10 and August 16, 2016, it could be determined obviously that this decision has not been followed by the state institutions in the affected area. Hundreds of buildings have been destroyed, roads have been broadened, areas have been erased and squares created and schools have been turned into police/military posts. The wide roads now connect these police/military posts. By conducting the demolition under the observation of the local personnel of the directorate of the Ministry for Culture and Tourism it has been aimed to give a legitimate situation. The demolition actions, which have violated the Urban Conservation Plan and the World Heritage Site Management Plan, have been conducted without the permission of the responsible municipality, responsible for enforcing these plans, and the information of the Site Management. Suriçi as an urban conservation site is object to the Law on the Conservation of Cultural Assets (No. 2863) and as part of the World Heritage Site under the conservation of international laws. For the destruction of any registered buildings, it is necessary that;

1) from the Conservation Board of Cultural Assets for each monument separately a decision is taken which states the imminent danger of collapse,

2) the technical personnel of the directorate for construction control at the relevant municipality prepare a report permitting the demolition of each individual building,

---

[80] Nevin Soyukaya, Archaeologist, Former head of the UNESCO World Heritage Site "DIYARBAKIR FORTRESS AND HEVSEL GARDENS CULTURAL LANDSCAPE", DAMAGE ASSESSMENT REPORT, Conflict Period and following Demolition of the Old city (SURİÇİ) of DIYARBAKIR, August 1, 2017

which state a risk for life and propriety, according to the Article 39 of the Law on Zoning (Town Planning) numbered 3194.

3) after the documentation on the claimed risk of collapse the relevant commission of the city council approves the demolition.

However, for the demolished buildings in the blockaded neighbourhoods, neither any technical assessment has been made nor any required permissions have been obtained from the Conservation Council for Cultural Assets and the relevant municipality. Today the actions and procedure continue which violate the national and international rules and regulations and lead to further destruction of the affected area. Without any design of surveys, restoration and restitution plans for the affected registered buildings, the remainings of qualitative building elements have been excavated with heavy equipment and dumped outside of Surici by personnel which have no expertise on this subject."

Nevin Soyukaya [81] concludes: *"The destruction of historical Suriçi took place in two different periods. The first was the period of armed conflict lasting from 9 September 2015 to 10 March 2016, the second period is characterized by systematic demolition and annihilation started on March 10, 2016 after the stop of the state operations an still continues.*
In the first stage heavy weapons, artillery, tanks, bombs and explosives were used. But the irreversible damage was inflicted in the second stage when demolition and excavations uprooted even the foundations of the buildings."

The Turkish State and its operatives have therefore committed the war crime as defined in art. 8 2 (e) (iv) of the Rome Statute of intentionally directing attacks against buildings dedicated to religion, education, art, science or charitable purposes, historic monuments,… not being military objectives.

---

[81] Nevin Soyukaya, Archaeologist, Former head of the UNESCO World Heritage Site "DIYARBAKIR FORTRESS AND HEVSEL GARDENS CULTURAL LANDSCAPE", DAMAGE ASSESSMENT REPORT, Conflict Period and following Demolition of the Old city (SURİÇİ) of DIYARBAKIR, August 1, 201, p. 11

US Nuclear Posture

James Mattis et al

In the first weeks of his Administration, President Trump ordered the Department of Defense to conduct a review of US nuclear weapons and strategies. The resultant Nuclear Posture Review, with its emphasis on smaller, 'useable' nukes, was published in February 2018. We reprint some key excerpts.

Secretary's Preface

Secretary of Defense James Mattis

'For decades, the United States led the world in efforts to reduce the role and number of nuclear weapons … During this time, the US nuclear weapons stockpile drew down by more than 85 percent from its Cold War high. Many hoped conditions had been set for even deeper reductions in global nuclear arsenals, and, ultimately, for their elimination.

While Russia initially followed America's lead … it retained large numbers of non-strategic nuclear weapons. Today, Russia is modernizing these weapons as well as its other strategic systems. Even more troubling has been Russia's adoption of military strategies and capabilities that rely on nuclear escalation for their success.' (Page I)

'This review rests on a bedrock truth: nuclear weapons have and will continue to play a critical role in deterring nuclear attack and in preventing large-scale conventional warfare between nuclear-armed states for the foreseeable future. US nuclear weapons not only defend our allies against conventional and nuclear threats, they also help them avoid the need to develop their own nuclear arsenals. This, in turn, furthers global security.' (Page III)

Executive Summary

An Evolving and Uncertain International Security Environment

'While the United States has continued to

reduce the number and salience of nuclear weapons, others, including Russia and China, have moved in the opposite direction. They have added new types of nuclear capabilities to their arsenals, increased the salience of nuclear forces in their strategies and plans, and engaged in increasingly aggressive behaviour, including in outer space and cyber space.' (Page V)

'The United States does not wish to regard either Russia or China as an adversary and seeks stable relations with both ... The United States and Russia have in the past maintained strategic dialogues to manage nuclear competition and nuclear risks. Given Russian actions, including its occupation of Crimea, this constructive engagement has declined substantially. We look forward to conditions that would once again allow for transparent and constructive engagement with Russia.' (Page VI)

Deterrence of Nuclear and Non-Nuclear Attacks

'Effective US deterrence of nuclear attack and non-nuclear strategic attack requires ensuring that potential adversaries do not miscalculate regarding the consequences of nuclear first use, either regionally or against the United States itself. They must understand that there are no possible benefits from non-nuclear aggression or limited nuclear escalation. Correcting any such misperceptions is now critical to maintaining strategic stability in Europe and Asia.' (Page VII)

The Triad: Present and Future

'The current non-strategic nuclear force consists exclusively of a relatively small number of B61 gravity bombs carried by F-15E and allied dual capable aircraft (DCA). The United States is incorporating nuclear capability onto the forward-deployable, nuclear capable F-35 as a replacement for the current ageing DCA. In conjunction with the XI NUCLEAR POSTURE REVIEW ongoing life extension program for the B61 bomb, it will be a key contributor to continued regional deterrence stability and the assurance of allies.' (Pages X-XI)

Enhancing Deterrence with Non-Strategic Nuclear Capabilities

'... To meet the emerging requirements of US strategy, the United States will now pursue select supplements to the replacement program to enhance the flexibility and responsiveness of US nuclear forces ... These supplements will enhance deterrence by denying potential adversaries any mistaken confidence that limited nuclear employment can provide a useful advantage over the United States and its allies. Russia's belief that limited nuclear first use, potentially including low-yield weapons, can provide such an advantage is based, in part, on Moscow's perception that its greater number and variety of non-strategic nuclear systems provide a coercive advantage in crises and at lower levels of conflict ... To address these types of challenges and preserve deterrence stability, the United States will enhance the flexibility and range of its tailored deterrence options. To be clear, this is not intended to, nor does it enable, 'nuclear war-fighting'. Expanding flexible US nuclear options now, to include low-yield options, is important for the preservation of credible deterrence against regional aggression. It will raise the nuclear threshold and help ensure that potential adversaries perceive no possible advantage in limited nuclear escalation, making nuclear employment less likely ... [I]n the near-term, the United States will modify a small number of existing SLBM [submarine launched ballistic missile] warheads to provide a low-yield option, and in the longer term, pursue a modern nuclear-armed sea-launched cruise missile (SLCM). Unlike DCA [dual capable aircraft], a low-yield SLBM warhead and SLCM will not require or rely on host nation support to provide deterrent effect. They will provide additional diversity in platforms, range, and survivability, and a valuable hedge against future nuclear 'break out' scenarios.

Department of Defense and National Nuclear Security Administration (NNSA) will develop for deployment a low-yield SLBM warhead to ensure a prompt response option that is able to penetrate adversary defences ... In addition to this near-term step, for the longer term the United States will pursue a nuclear-armed SLCM, leveraging existing technologies to help ensure its cost effectiveness. SLCM will provide a needed non-strategic regional presence, an assured response capability. It also will provide an arms control compliant response to Russia's non-compliance with the Intermediate-range Nuclear Forces Treaty, its non-strategic nuclear arsenal, and its other destabilizing behaviours. (Pages XI-XIII)

Non-Proliferation and Arms Control

'Russia continues to violate a series of arms control treaties and commitments. In the nuclear context, the most significant Russian violation involves a system banned by the Intermediate-range Nuclear Forces Treaty. In a broader context, Russia is either rejecting or avoiding its obligations and commitments under numerous agreements, and has rebuffed US efforts to follow the New Strategic Arms Reduction Treaty (START) with another round of negotiated reductions and to pursue reductions in non-strategic nuclear forces.' (Page XVII)

II. An Evolving and Uncertain International Security Environment

Russia

'Russia considers the United States and the North Atlantic Treaty Organization (NATO) to be the principal threats to its contemporary geopolitical ambitions. Russian strategy and doctrine emphasize the potential coercive and military uses of nuclear weapons. It mistakenly assesses that the threat of nuclear escalation or actual first use of nuclear weapons would serve to 'de-escalate' a conflict on terms favourable to Russia. These mistaken perceptions increase the prospect for dangerous miscalculation and escalation. Russia has sought to enable the implementation of its strategy and doctrine through a comprehensive modernization of its nuclear arsenal. Russia's strategic nuclear modernization has increased, and will continue to increase its warhead delivery capacity, and provides Russia with the ability to rapidly expand its deployed warhead numbers. In addition to modernizing 'legacy' Soviet nuclear systems, Russia is developing and deploying new nuclear warheads and launchers ...

These theatre- and tactical-range systems are not accountable under the New START Treaty and Russia's non-strategic nuclear weapons modernization is increasing the total number of such weapons in its arsenal, while significantly improving its delivery capabilities. This includes the production, possession, and flight testing of a ground-launched cruise missile in violation of the INF Treaty. Moscow believes these systems may provide useful options for escalation advantage. Finally, despite Moscow's frequent criticism of US missile defence, Russia is also modernizing its long-standing nuclear-armed ballistic missile defence system and designing a new ballistic missile defence interceptor.

Russia's increased reliance on nuclear capabilities to include coercive threats, nuclear modernization programs, refusal to negotiate any limits on its non-strategic nuclear forces, and its decision to violate the INF Treaty and other commitments all clearly indicate that Russia has rebuffed repeated US efforts to reduce the salience, role, and number of nuclear weapons. (Pages 8 – 10)

Uncertainties

'There are two forms of uncertainty regarding the future security environment which US nuclear policy, strategy, and posture must take into account. The first is geopolitical uncertainty. This includes the potential for rapid shifts in how other states view the United States, its allies, and partners; changing alignments among other states; and relative power shifts in the international system ...The second form of uncertainty is technological. This includes the potential for unanticipated technological breakthroughs in the application of existing technologies, or the development of wholly new technologies, that change the nature of the threats we face and the capabilities required to address them effectively.' (Page 14)

VI. US Strategies to Counter Contemporary Threats

A Tailored Strategy for Russia

'Russia is not the Soviet Union and the Cold War is long over. However, despite our best efforts to sustain a positive relationship, Russia now perceives the United States and NATO as its principal opponent and impediment to realizing its destabilizing geopolitical goals in Eurasia ... Most concerning are Russia's national security policies, strategy, and doctrine that include an emphasis on the threat of limited nuclear escalation, and its continuing development and fielding of increasingly diverse and expanding nuclear capabilities ... Effective US deterrence of Russian nuclear attack and non-nuclear strategic attack now requires ensuring that the Russian leadership does not miscalculate regarding the consequences of limited nuclear first-use, either regionally or against the United States itself. Russia must instead understand that nuclear first-use, however limited, will fail to achieve its objectives, fundamentally alter the nature of a conflict, and trigger incalculable and intolerable costs for Moscow. Our strategy will ensure Russia understands that any use of nuclear weapons, however limited, is unacceptable ... This strategy will ensure Russia understands it has no advantages in will [sic], non-nuclear capabilities, or nuclear escalation options that enable it to anticipate a possible benefit from non-nuclear aggression or limited nuclear escalation. Correcting any Russian misperceptions along these lines is important to maintaining deterrence in Europe and strategic stability ... To correct any Russian misperceptions of advantage and credibly deter Russian nuclear or non-nuclear strategic attacks—which could now include attacks against U.S. NC3—the President must have a range of limited and graduated options, including a variety of delivery systems and explosive yields.' (Pages 30 – 31)

VII. Current and Future US Nuclear Capabilities

Enhancing Deterrence with Non-Strategic Nuclear Capabilities

'Existing elements of the nuclear force replacement program predate the dramatic deterioration of the strategic environment. To meet the emerging requirements of US strategy, the United States will now pursue select supplements to the replacement program to enhance the flexibility and responsiveness of US nuclear forces. It is a reflection of the versatility and flexibility of the US triad that only modest supplements are now required in this much more challenging threat environment … Recent Russian statements on this evolving nuclear weapons doctrine appear to lower the threshold for Moscow's first-use of nuclear weapons. Russia demonstrates its perception of the advantage these systems provide through numerous exercises and statements. Correcting this mistaken Russian perception is a strategic imperative. North Korea is illicitly developing a range of strategic and non-strategic nuclear systems to threaten the United States, allies, and partners. It may mistakenly perceive that these systems, when coupled with the threat of a strategic nuclear attack against the United States, would provide advantageous nuclear escalation options in crises or conflict …

For decades, the United States has deployed low-yield nuclear options to strengthen deterrence and assurance. Expanding flexible US nuclear options now, to include low-yield options, is important for the preservation of credible deterrence against regional aggression. To be clear, this is not intended to enable, nor does it enable, 'nuclear war-fighting'. Nor will it lower the nuclear threshold. Rather, expanding US tailored response options will raise the nuclear threshold and help ensure that potential adversaries perceive no possible advantage in limited nuclear escalation, making nuclear weapons employment less likely.

Consequently, the United States will maintain, and enhance as necessary, the capability to forward deploy nuclear bombers and Dual Capable Aircraft around the world. We are committed to upgrading DCA with the nuclear-capable F-35 aircraft. We will work with NATO to best ensure—and improve where needed—the readiness, survivability, and operational effectiveness of DCA based in Europe ... DoD and NNSA will develop for deployment a low-yield SLBM warhead to ensure a prompt response option that is able to penetrate adversary defences. This is a comparatively low-cost and near-term modification to an existing capability that will help counter any mistaken perception of an exploitable 'gap' in US regional deterrence capabilities. Doing so will not increase the number of deployed US ballistic missile warheads, as the low yield weapons will replace higher-yield weapons currently deployed.

In addition to this near-term step, for the longer term the United States will pursue a nuclear-armed submarine launched cruise missile, leveraging existing technologies to help ensure its cost effectiveness. SLCM will provide a needed non-strategic regional presence, an assured response capability, and an INF-Treaty compliant response to Russia's continuing Treaty violation. If Russia returns to compliance with its arms control obligations, reduces its non-strategic nuclear arsenal, and corrects its other destabilizing behaviours, the United States may reconsider the pursuit of a SLCM ... Given the increasing need for flexible and low-yield options to strengthen deterrence and assurance, we will immediately begin efforts to restore this capability by initiating a capabilities study leading to an Analysis of Alternatives (AoA) for the rapid development of a modern SLCM.' (Pages 52 – 55)

Full text available at: https://bit.ly/2nDa4Rw

China rejects 'cold-war mentality'

The 2018 NPR describes China as 'a major challenge to US interests in Asia,' and outlines a strategy to 'prevent Beijing from mistakenly concluding that it could secure an advantage through the limited use of its theater nuclear capabilities or that any use of nuclear weapons, however limited, is acceptable'.

In response, Defense Ministry spokesman Ren Guoqiang, said 'We hope the U.S. side will discard its 'cold-war mentality,' shoulder its own special and primary responsibility for nuclear disarmament, understand correctly China's strategic intentions and take a fair view on China's national defense and military development'.

The boat we're in

Vladimir Putin

On 1 March 2018, President Putin discussed Russia's security and defence in the final part of his address to the Federal Assembly, from which these excerpts are taken.

… I will speak about the newest systems of Russian strategic weapons that we are creating in response to the unilateral withdrawal of the United States of America from the Anti-Ballistic Missile (ABM) Treaty and the practical deployment of their missile defence systems both in the US and beyond their national borders … Back in 2000, the US announced its withdrawal from the Anti-Ballistic Missile Treaty. Russia was categorically against this. We saw the Soviet-US ABM Treaty, signed in 1972, as the cornerstone of the international security system. Under this treaty, the parties had the right to deploy ballistic missile defence systems only in one of its regions. Russia deployed these systems around Moscow, and the US around its Grand Forks land-based inter-continental Ballistic missile (ICBM) base.

Together with the Strategic Arms Reduction Treaty (START), the ABM Treaty not only created an atmosphere of trust but also prevented either party from recklessly using nuclear weapons, which would have endangered humankind, because the limited number of ballistic missile defence systems made the potential aggressor vulnerable to a response strike. We did our best to dissuade the Americans from withdrawing from the Treaty. All in vain. The US pulled out of the Treaty in 2002. Even after that we tried to develop constructive dialogue with the Americans. We proposed working together in this area to ease concerns and maintain the atmosphere of trust. At one point, I thought that a compromise was possible, but this was not to be. All our proposals, absolutely all of them, were rejected. And then we said that we would have to improve our modern strike systems to protect our security. In reply, the US said that it is not creating a global Ballistic Missile Defence (BMD) system against Russia, which is free to do as it pleases, and that the US will presume that our actions are not spearheaded against the US.

The reasons behind this position are obvious. After the collapse of the USSR, Russia, which was known as the Soviet Union or Soviet Russia abroad, lost 23.8 per cent of its national territory, 48.5 per cent of its population, 41 per cent of its GDP, 39.4 per cent of its industrial potential (nearly half of our potential, I would underscore), as well as 44.6 per cent of its military capability due to the division of the Soviet Armed Forces among the former Soviet republics. The military equipment of the Russian army was becoming obsolete, and the Armed Forces were in a sorry state. A civil war was raging in the Caucasus, and US inspectors oversaw the operation of our leading uranium enrichment plants. For a certain time, the question was not whether we would be able to develop a strategic weapon system – some wondered if our country would even be able to safely store and maintain the nuclear weapons that we inherited after the collapse of the USSR. Russia had outstanding debts, its economy could not function without loans from the International Monetary Fund and the World Bank; the social sphere was impossible to sustain.

Apparently, our partners got the impression that it was impossible in the foreseeable historical perspective for our country to revive its economy, industry, defence industry and Armed Forces to levels supporting the necessary strategic potential. And if that is the case, there is no point in reckoning with Russia's opinion; it is necessary to pursue further the ultimate unilateral military advantage in order to dictate the terms in every sphere in the future. Basically, this position, this logic, judging from the realities of that period, is understandable, and we ourselves are to blame. All these years, the entire 15 years since the withdrawal of the United States from the Anti-Ballistic Missile Treaty, we have consistently tried to re-engage the American side in serious discussions, in reaching agreements in the sphere of strategic stability.

We managed to accomplish some of these goals. In 2010, Russia and the US signed the New START Treaty, containing measures for the further reduction and limitation of strategic offensive arms. However, in light of the plans to build a global anti-ballistic missile system, which are still being carried out today, all agreements signed within the framework of New START are now gradually being devalued, because while the number of carriers and weapons is being reduced, one of the parties, namely the US, is permitting constant, uncontrolled growth of the number of anti-ballistic missiles, improving their quality, and creating new missile launching areas. If we do not do something, eventually this will result in the complete devaluation of Russia's nuclear potential, meaning that all of our missiles could simply be intercepted.

Despite our numerous protests and pleas, the American machine has been set in motion, the conveyer belt moves forward. There are new missile defence systems installed in Alaska and California. As a result of NATO's expansion to the east, two new missile defence areas were created in Western Europe: one has already been established in Romania, while the deployment of the system in Poland is now almost complete. Their range will keep increasing; new launching areas are to be created in Japan and South Korea. The US global missile defence system also includes five cruisers and 30 destroyers, which, as far as we know, have been deployed to regions in close proximity to Russia's borders. I am not exaggerating in the least; and this work proceeds apace.

So, what have we done, apart from protesting and warning? How will Russia respond to this challenge? This is how. During all these years since the unilateral US withdrawal from the ABM Treaty, we have been working intensively on advanced equipment and arms, which allowed us to make a breakthrough in developing new models of strategic weapons. Let me recall that the United States is creating a global missile defence system primarily for countering strategic arms that follow ballistic trajectories. These weapons form the backbone of our nuclear deterrence forces, just like other members of the nuclear club. As such, Russia has developed, and works continuously to perfect, highly effective but modestly priced systems to overcome missile defence. They are installed on all of our intercontinental ballistic missile complexes.

In addition, we have embarked on the development of the next generation of missiles. For example, the Defence Ministry and enterprises of the missile and aerospace industry are in the active phase of testing a new missile system with a heavy intercontinental missile. We called it *Sarmat,* which will replace the *Voevoda* system made in the USSR. Its immense power was universally recognised … *Voevoda's* range is 11,000 km while *Sarmat* has practically no range restrictions … *Sarmat* is a formidable missile and, owing to its characteristics, is untroubled by even the most advanced missile defence systems. But we did not stop at that. We started to develop new types of strategic arms that do not use ballistic trajectories at all when moving towards a target and, therefore, missile defence systems are useless against them, absolutely pointless …

In late 2017, Russia successfully launched its latest nuclear-powered missile at the central training ground. During its flight, the nuclear-powered engine reached its design capacity and provided the necessary propulsion. Now that the missile launch and ground tests were successful, we can begin developing a completely new type of weapon, a strategic nuclear weapons system with a nuclear-powered missile … As you no doubt understand, no other country has developed anything like this. There will be something similar one day but by that time our guys will have come up with something even better.

Now, we all know that the design and development of unmanned weapon systems is another common trend in the world. As concerns Russia, we have developed unmanned submersible vehicles that can move at great depths (I would say extreme depths) inter-continentally, at a speed multiple times higher than the speed of submarines … Unmanned underwater vehicles can carry either conventional or nuclear warheads, which enables them to engage various targets, including aircraft groups, coastal fortifications and infrastructure …

Countries with high research potential and advanced technology are known to be actively developing so-called hypersonic weapons … Russia already has such a weapon. The most important stage in the development of modern weapons systems was the creation of a high-precision hypersonic aircraft missile system; as you already know for sure, it is the only one of its kind in the world …

I will say once again what we have repeatedly told our American and European partners who are NATO members: we will make the necessary efforts to neutralise the threats posed by the deployment of the US global missile defence system. We mentioned this during talks, and even said it publicly. Back in 2004, after the exercises of the strategic nuclear forces when the system was tested for the first time, I said the following at a meeting with the press …

'As other countries increase the number and quality of their arms and military potential, Russia will also need to ensure it has new generation weapons and technology. In this respect, I am pleased to inform you that successfully completed experiments during these exercises enable us to confirm that, in the near future, the Russian Armed Forces, the Strategic Missile Forces, will receive new hypersonic-speed, high-precision weapons systems that can hit targets at inter-continental distance and can adjust their altitude and course as they travel. This is a very significant statement because no country in the world as of now has such arms in their military arsenal.'

Of course, every word has a meaning because we are talking about the possibility of bypassing interception boundaries. Why did we do all this? Why did we talk about it? As you can see, we made no secret of our plans and spoke openly about them, primarily to encourage our partners to hold talks. Let me repeat, this was in 2004. It is actually surprising that, despite all the problems with the economy, finances and the defence industry, Russia has remained a major nuclear power. No, nobody really wanted to talk to us about the core of the problem, and nobody wanted to listen to us. So listen now ...

I want to emphasise specifically that the newly developed strategic arms – in fact, new types of strategic weapons – are not the result of something left over from the Soviet Union. Of course, we relied on some ideas from our ingenious predecessors. But everything I have described today is the result of the last several years, the product of dozens of research organisations, design bureaus and institutes ...

I hope that everything that was said today would make any potential aggressor think twice, since unfriendly steps against Russia, such as deploying missile defences and bringing NATO infrastructure closer to the Russian border, become ineffective in military terms and entail unjustified costs, making them useless for those promoting these initiatives.

It was our duty to inform our partners of what I said here today under the international commitments Russia had subscribed to. When the time comes, foreign and defence ministry experts will have many opportunities to discuss all these matters with them, if of course our partners so desire.

For my part, I should note that we have conducted the work to reinforce Russia's defence capability within the current arms control agreements; we are not violating anything. I should specifically say that Russia's growing military strength is not a threat to anyone; we have never had any plans to use this potential for offensive, let alone aggressive goals. We are not threatening anyone, not going to attack anyone, or take away anything from anyone with the threat of weapons. We do not need anything; just the opposite. I deem it necessary to emphasise (and it is very important) that Russia's growing military power is a solid guarantee of global peace, as this power preserves and will preserve strategic parity and the balance of forces in the world, which, as is known, have been and remain a key factor of international security after World War Two and up to the present day.

And to those who, in the past 15 years, have tried to accelerate an arms race and seek unilateral advantage against Russia, have introduced restrictions and sanctions that are illegal from the standpoint of international law aiming to restrain our nation's development, including in the military area, I will say this: everything you have tried to prevent through such a policy has already happened. No one has managed to restrain Russia.

Now we have to be aware of this reality and be sure that everything I have said today is not a bluff – and it is not a bluff, believe me – and to give it a thought, and dismiss those who live in the past and are unable to look into the future, to stop rocking the boat we are all in, which is called the Earth.

In this connection, I would like to note the following. We are greatly concerned by certain provisions of the revised nuclear posture review, which expand the opportunities for reducing, and reduce, the threshold for the use of nuclear arms. Behind closed doors, one may say anything to calm down anyone, but we read what is written. And what is written is that this strategy can be put into action in response to conventional arms attacks and even to a cyber-threat.

I should note that our military doctrine says Russia reserves the right to use nuclear weapons solely in response to a nuclear attack, or an attack with other weapons of mass destruction against the country or its allies, or an act of aggression against us with the use of conventional weapons that threaten the very existence of the state. This all is very clear and specific.

As such, I see it is my duty to announce the following. Any use of nuclear weapons against Russia or its allies, weapons of short, medium or any range at all, will be considered as a nuclear attack on this country. Retaliation will be immediate, with all the attendant consequences. There should be no doubt about this whatsoever. There is no need to create more threats to the world. Instead, let us sit down at the negotiating table and devise together a new and relevant system of international security and sustainable development for human civilisation. We have been saying this all along. All these proposals are still valid. Russia is ready for this.

Our policies will never be based on claims to 'exceptionalism'. We protect our interests and respect the interests of other countries. We observe international law and believe in the inviolable central role of the UN. These are the principles and approaches that allow us to build strong, friendly and equal relations with the absolute majority of countries. Our comprehensive strategic partnership with the People's Republic of China is one example. Russia and India also enjoy a special privileged strategic relationship. Our relations with many other countries in the world are entering a new dynamic stage …

This is a turning period for the entire world and those who are willing and able to change, those who are taking action and moving forward, will take the lead. Russia and its people have expressed this will at every defining moment in our history. In just 30 years, we have undergone changes that took centuries in other countries ...

http://en.kremlin.ru/events/president/news/56957

Russia in six years

Zhores Medvedev
Roy Medvedev

Zhores A. Medvedev is a biochemist, gerontologist and historian who has lived in London since the 1970s. His books include The Rise and Fall of TD Lysenko, Nuclear Disaster in the Urals, The Legacy of Chernobyl, Gorbachev, The Unknown Stalin *(together with RA Medvedev), and* Nutrition and Longevity.

Roy Alexandrovich Medvedev is a historian and former People's Deputy of the USSR and Deputy of the Supreme Soviet of the USSR, 1989-1991. He lives in Moscow. His many books include The October Revolution, Let History Judge: The origins and consequences of Stalinism, Political Essays, The Samizdat Register, *and* Post-Soviet Russia: A journey through the Yeltsin era.

They were born in Tiflis in 1925.

Great Breakthrough

On 1 March 2018 in his pre-election address to the Federal Assembly, Vladimir Putin promised Russia a 'Great Breakthrough':

' ... the speed of technological change is growing rapidly, going up sharply. Those who use this technological wave will break far ahead. Those who cannot do this, the wave will simply overwhelm, drown.'

The same thought was clearly expressed in his Inauguration speech of 7 May, elected again as president for the next six years, when he repeated his pre-election promise of an 'economic, technological breakthrough ...'

Not only as historians, but also as people who have lived long lives, we remember the words of another Russian-Soviet leader, similar in meaning, taking into account the time, uttered on 4 February 1931 at the All-Union Conference of Workers of Socialist Industry:

'We are 50 to 100 years behind the advanced countries. We must run this distance in ten years. Either we do it or we are dashed.'

This grandiose programme was carried out with great tension by two five-year plans according to a compulsory and detailed plan, the implementation of which was the law and priority for the entire country. During ten years, thousands of new factories and industrial plants were commissioned: factories, mines and power plants. Peasant Russia was transformed into an industrial power.

During the 20th century, we witnessed several successful economic breakthroughs. There was Franklin Roosevelt's 'New Deal' in 1933-1938, which raised the United States from the devastation of the economic crisis and the 'Great Depression'. During the years from 1946 to 1950, Germany and Japan revived rapidly from the ruins of defeat in World War Two. Restoration of the economies of France, The Netherlands, Belgium and Norway, fragmented and plundered after their occupation in 1940, relied on the generous assistance of the Marshall Plan, announced by the United States in 1947.

Programmes of economic breakthrough were not always successful. Mao Zedong's 'Great Leap Forward', started in China in 1958, turned into a disaster for the people of that great country. In 1957, Khrushchev's programme for agriculture, entitled 'Catch up and outstrip America', ended in failure. Everyone remembers the sad fate of Gorbachev's *Perestroika*. During the 1990s, 'shock therapy' programmes failed; voucher privatization, pledge auctions for the distribution of state property to private owners and, finally, the 'GKO' financial pyramid, which led to default, were attempts at a breakthrough from socialism to capitalism undertaken by Boris Yeltsin. They brought down the welfare of the population and the economy of the whole country. President Putin's 'big breakthrough' has a better chance of success, although not all of his promises can be realized in such a short time. The developed and mandatory economic programme of new reforms is not yet available. The presidential decree 'On national goals and strategic tasks for the development of the Russian Federation for the period until 2024', signed on 7 May, is not a strict mandatory plan, supported by finance, concrete projects and economic calculations, but only intentions and instructions to the government.

Economic realities and breakthroughs

Economic programmes and human factors in 'breakthroughs', as we know, are not the same thing. Peter the Great, who raised Russia's industrial potential to unprecedented heights, achieved this through violence and coercion of serfs and all other classes of society. The economic and military power of the empire increased, while the standard of living of the population, which did not exceed 20-25 million people in the period 1700-1725, declined.

Economic transformation during 'Stalin's five year plans' was achieved by coercion and mass repression. The development of large-scale industry occurred on the basis of violence and expropriations, the most famous of which were 'dekulakization' of wealthy peasants and confiscation of financial resources and property of small entrepreneurs who created thousands of useful and successful industries and trade enterprises in the consumer sector during the period of New Economic Policy (NEP) from 1922 to 1929. Many factories, including the legendary Moscow Automobile ZIS and the Stalingrad and Chelyabinsk Tractor Plants, were created through comprehensive importation of equipment from the US and under the guidance of American engineers.

'New Deal' Roosevelt was a success in the United States, thanks to government intervention in economic projects. To eliminate unemployment, a shortened 35-hour work week was legislatively introduced and an extensive programme of public works was launched, primarily on the construction of highways, railways and bridges. The dollar gold standard was abolished. The government could print any sums of dollars not backed by gold. A minimum wage for workers was introduced. This limited period of state socialism proved salutary for American capitalism.

The failures of other 'breakthroughs' also have objective explanations. Mao Zedong's 'great leap forward' ended in failure as it had no technical programme, nor were there sufficient financial, material and human resources. The same applies to Gorbachev's 'restructuring'.

The historical load carried by Russian science and technology

The first electronic computer was built in the United States in 1945. At the same time in the Soviet Union, cybernetics was declared bourgeois and idealistic pseudoscience. The division of many scientific branches into 'bourgeois' and 'socialist' continued until 1954. In computer technologies, the Soviet Union lagged behind the US for two technological generations. The last embargo on the sale of American computers to the Soviet Union was introduced by President Jimmy Carter in the 1980s. In the production and application of computer technology, Russia currently lags behind not only the US and Japan, but also China.

The collapse of the Soviet Union and the formation on its territory of 15 new states led to numerous discontinuities of the previously unified industrial economy and financial system. The scientific and creative intelligentsia suffered greatly from hyperinflation that arose in the Russian Federation in 1992. Funding of many scientific and technical developments was minimized or ceased altogether. Scientists' salaries were not indexed to inflation. Inevitably, mass emigration of scientists, primarily young people, started. The losses to science in Russia, a 'brain drain', are estimated as hundreds of thousands of scientists. Soviet specialists in the fields of nuclear and missile technology, especially from the former union republics, found application in the development of these industries in India, Pakistan, North Korea, Israel, Iran and some other countries.

In Russia since 2000, on the other hand, there has been immigration of scientists from many Commonwealth of Independent States (CIS) countries, primarily Ukraine, Belarus, Kazakhstan, Georgia and Armenia. Millions of qualified specialists and workers, not only Russians who left CIS countries, helped to increase the scientific, technical and industrial potential of the Russian Federation in many important sectors. However, in the newest digital technologies, which until recently had a global character and spread independently of state borders, Russia, with the signs of a new Cold War and the introduction of various embargoes, discovered many problems. The 'breakthrough' programme should, first of all, ensure the independence of Russia and its allies from numerous sanctions and provocations, which have been growing since 2014.

Financial resources for the breakthrough

Any programme that envisages an increase in the wellbeing of the population, an increase in the birth rate and life expectancy, an increase in maternity benefits, and the growth of pensions for the elderly and disabled, the development of medical care, education and science, and the improvement of urban ecology requires extensive additional budgetary financing and accelerated growth in the production and export sectors of the economy. The same applies to developing transport routes. The budgets already approved by the State Duma for 2018-2020 have not promised a 'breakthrough' and were in deficit. Borrowings in foreign financial markets were envisaged.

Taking into account President Putin's new directives, it is planned to revise the budget for 2019, the revenue and expense items of which will be significantly increased. The current rise in world oil prices creates favourable conditions for this. Traditional methods of increasing budget revenues are common to all countries and they will undoubtedly be applied in Russia. First and foremost, the variety of taxes on income, sales, profits and property are increased. Additional budgetary funds will be released by increasing the retirement age, which is at present 55 years for women and

60 for men, the lowest in Europe.

Traditionally, increased budget revenues are achieved by higher prices for gasoline and diesel fuel, as well as for tobacco and alcohol. Subsidies for utilities will be abolished. Reducing military spending and assistance programmes to other states could provide Russia with additional substantial funds. Import substitution, started in 2014, will be expanded. In 2019, it is planned to put into operation new gas pipelines and increase gas exports, both to the West and to the East.

Other measures specific to Russia will also be used. First of all, there are special measures for the return of many billions of capital, which leaked to offshore and Western banks during the period of 'oligarchic' capitalism. This was not stopped even after 2000. Administrative expenses will also be significantly reduced; the vast apparatus at presidential, governmental and governors' levels will be reduced.

Putin's special reserves

Having been in power for almost 18 years, President Putin has constantly increased personal power and responsibility, preserving and even increasing throughout this time a high level of trust and support in Russian society. With Khrushchev, Brezhnev, Gorbachev and Yeltsin, everything was the other way round. The same can be said about Western leaders, especially American and British. In the modern world, the increase in the trust rating, with long terms of office, is demonstrated only by Xi Jinping in China, Nazarbayev in Kazakhstan, and Lukashenko in Belarus. Putin has not defined his ideology, besides emphasising his patriotism. He strengthened the influence of the Orthodox Church, but not at the expense of other religions. He encourages moderate Islam in Russia and in the Islamic autonomous areas of Russia. Putin was the first Russian leader to visit the main Catholic cathedral and the Old Believer temple in Moscow. He has repeatedly expressed respect for Judaism and Buddhism. In this respect the contrast between Putin and Donald Trump is quite obvious.

The main opposition to Putin is the oligarchs. However, their influence continues to decline. In 2000, 70 per cent of the Russian economy was controlled by oligarchic capitalism and only 30 per cent by the government. By 2018, the public sector of the economy dominated and acquired a more dynamic corporate structure. However, a significant number of young people, not familiar with the problems of even the recent past, and brought up with the internet and social networks, relate very coolly to Putin's policy. Opposition to Putin from this side, however, has little creative potential. The communist and liberal oppositions have weak electoral support and do not offer alternative programmes.

The tasks set by Putin for the next six years are so great that they will only be solved by directly attracting private capital. This was how the Winter Olympics in Sochi in 2014 were financed; two-thirds of the costs for construction of the facilities were covered by private investment. The construction of the grandiose Crimean bridge across the Kerch Strait, started in 2015, is carried out by private equity company, Stroigazmontazh, the main shareholder of which is the oligarch Arkady Rotenberg. Construction of new high-speed railways is carried out by international consortia.

To implement major construction projects during the period 2018-2024, design offices with responsible administrators will be established, with extraordinary powers and working independently of the government and the state budget. In the same way, preparations were made for the 2018 World Cup. Over 70 per cent of these multibillion-dollar expenditures are extrabudgetary funds. But they will be returned. Investments by FIFA, the International Federation of Football Associations, and the flow of football fans and tourists make significant contributions to the economy of cities, both financial and political. The resultant infrastructures become state property.

Russia is now a young, new, yet ancient country. Unlike Lenin, who created the Soviet Union, tearing the country away from its 'imperial' past, Putin dates the history of the new Russia from Kievan Rus, its baptism in 988, or maybe even earlier. Most Western and world leaders, while defining their policy towards the Russian Federation, do not understand this. This is not understood by many Russian citizens. But for Russian historians this is already obvious.

Patriotic outlook, extending to the masses, unites many people around common spiritual and historical values. Russia is not only a state, but also an independent civilization, one of several, Chinese, Japanese, Arab, Indian and others surviving in the world. The independent French, German-Austrian, English, Greek, Spanish and other civilizations in the past have merged into a common 'Western' civilization in the last decades.

2024 is defined as a control, only because it coincides with the completion of the term of office of the Russian president elected in May 2018. However, it cannot be ruled out that with the success of a 'breakthrough', not even fully, Putin's powers could be extended. Examples from China, Kazakhstan, Belarus and Azerbaijan show that changes in constitutions are easier to accomplish than a change of power. But the main condition for such a scenario for the future is the success of the programme for improving people's welfare.

Spokesman Books: Jo Vellacott Titles

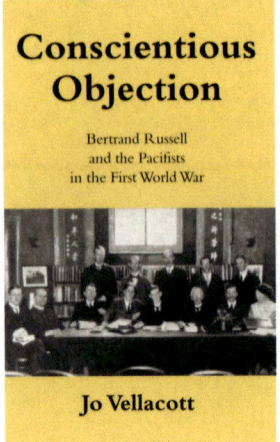

Conscientious Objection:
Bertrand Russell and the Pacifists in the First World War

This story of the No-Conscription Fellowship (NCF) focuses o
Bertrand Russell's contribution, it has been recognised a
contributing to an understanding of how the NCF was made u
how it worked, its successes and failures, and dissensions within i
particularly over the acceptability of various forms of alternativ
service and of political action in the cause of peace.

Price: £14.99 | 340 pages | Paperback | ISBN: 978 0 85124 842

From Liberal to Labour with Women's Suffrage *The Story of Catherine Marshall*

Catherine Marshall was a vital figure in the women's suffrage
movement in Britain before the First World War. Using her
remarkable political skills on behalf of the major non-militant
organization, the National Union of Women's Suffrage Societies,
she built close connections with major suffragist politicians,
leading some - in all three parties - to consider adopting a measure
of women's enfranchisement as a party plank.

Price: £17.99 | 518 pages | Paperback | ISBN: 978 0 85124 8523

Living and Learning in Peace and War

This is a memoir of the first twenty-five years of a long life. Jo
Vellacott's early years were lived under the shadow still cast by the
First World War, but at a time when it was still possible to hope
that it had indeed been the war to end all wars. Gradually the
skies darkened and the rise of Nazism came to threaten the world

Price: £10.99 | 190 pages | Paperback | ISBN: 978 0 85124 8707

www.spokesmanbooks.com

Envoys

Working for Peace in 1916

Jo Vellacott

In her 97ᵗʰ year, Jo Vellacott sends fresh insights into old conflicts. She is the author of Conscientious Objection: Bertrand Russell and the Pacifists *(£14.99) and* From Liberal to Labour with Women's Suffrage: The story of Catherine Marshall *(£17.99), both published by Spokesman.*

Once the First World War started there seemed to be no way to stop it. Casualties mounted, rhetoric escalated, leaders in the belligerent nations focused on victory, even to talk of peace was seen as treasonous.

The International Women's Congress held at The Hague in April 1915 was truly remarkable. Pulled together by a handful of women, all suffragists (but without the blessing of any major international organization), the Congress was attended by over a thousand women, from neutral nations, from both sides of the conflict, and from both shores of the Atlantic. Jane Addams, later a peace laureate, and already a widely respected feminist well known for her social work in Chicago, and for her public presence, agreed to serve as President.

The name chosen in 1915 for the organization formed at the congress was 'International Women's Committee for Permanent Peace' (IWCPP), although it would become better known by its later name, the Women's International League for Peace and Freedom (WILPF), under which name it is still active. The earlier name had significance at the time; this was not a simple 'Stop the War' initiative, but the beginning of an attempt to formulate principles of international relations that could undergird a lasting peace.

Scarcely a handful of the women who met at The Hague so much as had a vote, but all had given time and thought to how the basis of international relations could be improved. First, it was essential that the war must end in a just and negotiated peace. Recriminations and blame-laying for the present war were ruled out of order in their discussions. The hope was to see the settlement embody systemic changes designed to forestall future conflicts, and to set up a mechanism for peaceful resolution if they did occur.

Not surprisingly, the resolutions passed by the Congress show awareness of the special vulnerability of women in wartime, as well as of the need to include women in all decision-making, and emphasize the changes that they hoped political empowerment of women might effect. But notably, they do not dwell on the victimization or even the empowerment of women. They are not confined to what were then seen as 'women's issues' but show a mature grasp of both problems and solutions of international relations, focusing instead on drawing up a blueprint for a just and lasting peace.

The principles affirmed include: no transfer of territory without consent of the populace; denial of the right of conquest; democratic control of foreign policy; future disputes to be referred to arbitration or conciliation (enforced if necessary by sanctions); removal of private profit from the arms industry; and – of course – women to have equal political rights and international representation. Other resolutions urge the establishment of a permanent International Court of Justice (enlarging the function and powers of the existing court at The Hague), and the establishment of a permanent conference to further international co-operation.

The wish list is long. A century later these are still admirable goals; we have, perhaps with reason, diminished faith in the will of politicians to carry them forward.

The Congress deliberately stayed away from any demand for a quick end to the war. A draft resolution calling for a truce was quickly withdrawn, largely because of the hostile reaction it met with in the public press and among politicians. But clearly, an end to the war was the heartfelt wish of those gathered at The Hague, and they readily accepted a proposal suggesting a way towards this. Present among them was Julia Grace Wales, a young Canadian teaching at the University of Wisconsin, who had already sought long and intelligently to find a way to help turn the world from the tragic path it was on. As a Canadian she was a British citizen, but living in Wisconsin exposed her to open discussion of peace and war; and the considerable number of young Germans among her students helped her maintain a balanced perspective. Congress had recognised that the core difficulty in opening negotiations is that the side that believes itself to be on top at any given time sees no reason to negotiate, since it will soon be victorious and in a position to dictate; the side that is struggling thinks any peace overture or call for a truce will simply be seen by the enemy as an admission of weakness. Almost obsessed by the call she felt to find a way towards peace, Wales had recognised the centrality of this difficulty and already, before the Congress was even planned, had drafted a plan that might circumvent it. Embodied in a pamphlet called *International Plan for Continuous Mediation without Armistice*, Wales's idea rapidly gained support among peace people in the US. A similar plan had been advocated from the outbreak of the war by a Hungarian, Rosika Schwimmer, who was also at the Congress, and the voyage to The Hague had provided opportunity for further discussion.

Wales did not suggest solutions for any particular issues between the belligerent nations, but laid out a mechanism by which small steps could be taken towards addressing the issues. Her proposal was that a neutral country, or group of countries, would agree to set up an ongoing conference to receive proposals, even tentative or partial statements of war aims, from belligerents, on which a move towards resolution could begin, and should also be actively engaged in drawing up and submitting to the warring sides 'reasonable proposals as a basis of peace'. Because it would facilitate mediation without a call for armistice, the plan would enable a start to be made without either side appearing to show weakness, and had the potential to offer a viable way forward. At the Congress, Grace's plan was readily accepted and approved.

After a few short days, the work of the Congress was done. Understanding had greatly increased among the women present, and they could leave satisfied that excellent resolutions had been approved, including one agreeing to meet again when and where the peace conference that should end the war would be held.

But what satisfaction was there in suggesting solutions that the statesmen would not read, might indeed never hear of?

Rosika Schwimmer, for one, could not bear to see the good work of the Conference used only for propaganda among the already converted. In the last hours, she called on the women at the gathering to send envoys out to meet with heads of state and foreign ministers in both belligerent and neutral nations, carrying with them the Congress resolutions and the plan for continuous mediation. Dr Alice Hamilton, an American physician who would make a name for her work in occupational medicine, described how Schwimmer, the only delegate who 'could swing the Congress off its feet' made a final impassioned appeal and succeeded in having them 'pass the resolution which filled most of us with dismay ... that the resolutions passed by the Congress be presented by a committee to the various Powers'.

Despite some evidence that she shared the initial dismay at the boldness of the plan, Jane Addams gave no public sign of hesitancy, and accepted the expressed will of the gathering. She came to see it as a more than worthwhile attempt, and she gave it all she had, despite her own ill-health.

Plans were made and delegates chosen with remarkable speed and efficiency. Addams would lead the delegation of women from neutral nations that would visit the capitals of the belligerents, while women from the belligerent nations could be among the envoys to the neutrals, or at times to statesmen of their own countries. It was understood from the outset that the main focus of their visits would be to bring forward the plan for neutral mediation, although other principles of peace should be discussed. What developed, in the event, was a kind of unofficial shuttle diplomacy, where the women took the role of message-carriers – a role that could not have been taken by any man at that time – from one nation to another, and sometimes back again, exploring possibilities and sounding out official opinion.

Delegation to the belligerent capitals

Addams's fellow delegates to the war capitals were Aletta Jacobs of The Netherlands, and Rose Genoni of Italy. Frau van Wulfften Palthe (Netherlands) and the doubting Alice Hamilton travelled with them as unofficial companions, although it still seemed to Hamilton to be 'a singularly fool[ish] performance'.

Throughout their visits to the warring nations, Jane Addams and her fellow envoys were met with caution, but never with outright rejection. In England, the National Union of Women's Suffrage Societies (NUWSS) was divided over the issue of peace efforts, and gave no official support, but Catherine Marshall, former Parliamentary Secretary to the NUWSS, used her pre-war political contacts to set up interviews for Addams with Prime Minister Asquith and Sir Edward Grey, the Foreign Secretary, both of whom agreed, albeit with reluctance. Addams also met officially with Lord Robert Cecil and Lord Crewe, both cabinet ministers. When she lunched with Lloyd George, newly appointed as Minister of Munitions, at 11 Downing Street, she even found an opportunity to tweak his Welsh conscience. Mary Sheepshanks, herself an active pacifist, later wrote that when another guest left the room Lloyd George's mood changed: '"Last Sunday" he said, "I was in Paris planning increases of munitions with Albert Thomas. I heard the church bells ringing, and I said to myself 'is this the right thing to be doing on the Lord's Day?' "Well, Mr. Lloyd

George," said Miss Addams, "perhaps when these thoughts come we ought to listen to them".' Evidently, the incident stayed in Lloyd George's mind, even as he tried to brush it off: the following week 'Lloyd George said to his guests, "Who do you think I had here last week? Jane Addams trying to convert me to pacifism!"'

The British statesmen did not close the door, despite their caution in the choice of words. Sir Edward Grey wondered aloud whether the neutral nations would hold off from action until the whole of Europe had been destroyed, although he is also reported to have said that if anything at all was said about the belligerents being willing to consider peace negotiations, he would deny it even if 'every word was true'. Lord Crewe, acting Foreign Minister at the time, rejected the word 'accept' as too strong for the attitude the British government would take towards the formation of a Neutral Conference, but he made the crucial statement, on paper, that they 'would not place any obstacles in the way of the formation of such a body or make any protest against its existence if it should come into being'.

Meeting with major leaders was not all that was expected of the envoys. In every country peace activists provided what opportunity they could for the envoys to meet with politicians and potential supporters. In England in particular, the programme followed by Addams was daunting. A list dated 'June 26?' and headed 'People we saw in England the last week for short half an hour' contains 48 individual names, not including '180 members of English Committee, Settlement people, etc. etc.' Included are Members of both Houses of Parliament, senior journalists and other writers, bishops, and many well known people, and the list is, to my knowledge from other sources, by no means complete.

Addams painted a vivid picture of the major players among the Central Powers. The German Foreign Minister, von Jagow, told the women that 'this is what women *ought* to do, and he couldn't understand why they hadn't done it sooner'. He also pointed out, reasonably, that acceptance of any US intervention was made more difficult by the shipment of American arms to the Allies. He even suggested that now was the time to go ahead, since neither side had an advantage.

The envoys saw a very human side of the German Chancellor, Bethmann von Hollweg, who had himself lost a son. Addams reported that 'He said nations at war *can't* begin negotiations, and he thought neutral nations had been too feeble – they should have taken a stronger line at once'. At the same time, he had 'slammed England' for her lack of understanding of Germany, and for her avowed determination to crush

Germany utterly, claiming (rather implausibly) that he never heard Germans saying that they wanted to crush England. Overall, Addams felt that the Chancellor was a good man, anxious to find a way out.

In Austria, the envoys found the suffering caused by the conflict already tragically visible; there were wounded soldiers everywhere, and a shortage of wheat had brought widespread hardship. Their meeting with the Prime Minister, Karl von Sturgkh, proved to be one of the highlights of the journey. After they had introduced their scheme, Addams, never over-confident, said apologetically that perhaps their mission might seem very foolish to him. His response was emphatic: 'He banged his fist on the table. "Foolish?" he said. "Not at all. Those are the first sensible words that have been uttered in this room for ten months. ... Men are fools! For nine months they've come to me in this room asking for more men and more money, and now at last you come with a reasonable proposal and ask for negotiations".' Count von Burian, Minister of Foreign Affairs, stressed the need for a forceful move to implement the proposed conference as soon as possible: the neutrals, he said, must not ask '"may we negotiate?" but must come with definite proposals again and again. And they *must not* wait.' The more countries came into the war, the more difficult it would become.

Visits to Allied countries were more difficult and discouraging than those to the Central Powers. The French Foreign Minister, Delcassé, whose country was, with Belgium, suffering the burden of invasion, treated them personally with courtesy. His picture of what was going on was a mirror image of what Germany was saying about the Allies, but he seemed to the envoys to be 'what you call a Jingo,' declaring that France would accept no terms until Germany was rendered incapable of aggression for a hundred years, which he said had to be done even if it cost France two men for every German life lost. He claimed that German resources were nearly at an end; Addams and her companions meanwhile had seen no signs of serious shortage in their visit to Germany, though they had in Austria. Only in France was the deputation 'followed everywhere by the police,' and they made little progress in what talks they had with Mlle Schlumberger, President of the French Suffrage Society. France was the only major belligerent from which no delegates had made their way to the Congress in April. Soon, however, other French suffragists would form a branch of the ICWPP, and issue a manifesto of support for the Hague Congress.

The visit of the delegation to the Belgian government, in exile at Le Havre in France, brought 'the first disagreeable experiences with the police,' other than being 'followed everywhere,' and having 'to be extremely careful' throughout the whole visit to France. In Le Havre the police officer objected to the Resolutions they were carrying, and said that they should have been censored, and the hotel where they had booked refused to take them in. But this mattered less to them than that M. d'Avignon, the Belgian Foreign Minister, met with them and admitted that a negotiated peace would be preferable to having the land fought over all over again. All the Belgians they met with wanted more than anything to get back to their own country; any kind of indemnity payment was less important for them. And even Belgium still had its pacifists; before leaving The Hague, Grace Wales had a long conversation with Mr Otlet, a leading Belgian pacifist who had years of work behind him in facilitating international federations of a variety of organizations, and who was eager to express his support of the plan for a conference of neutrals.

Italy came into the war on the Allied side while the delegation was on its way, so the Envoys who had planned to visit it as a neutral nation found themselves instead visiting a nation at war, and Rose Genoni had to leave them. Not surprisingly, the visit was discouraging; they were met with all the excitement and propaganda of early war involvement, not yet tempered by the realities of death and destruction. The War Ministry struck Jane Addams as 'boyish and pleased with their new toy'. The women did, however, add a long unplanned meeting with the Pope, and found him not only 'deeply distressed' by the war, but ready to have the Vatican take a part if a neutral conference of mediators should be formed.

The other delegation, consisting of Emily Balch, Chrystal Macmillan and Cor Ramondt-Hirschmann also interrupted their visits with the neutral nations to take a demanding three-day journey to Petrograd, where, after a delay of more than a week, they had an hour-long meeting with Sergei Sazonov, the Russian Foreign Minister. Their conversation ranged widely over a number of the issues dividing the nations. Sazonov blamed Germany for the war and took every opportunity to boost Russia's image. Less open than he seemed, he claimed that Russia had no further territorial ambitions – the envoys did not know that he had already concluded secret agreements with Britain and France to take over Turkish territory. As was their pattern, the envoys asked how he would respond to a conference of neutrals – would he see this as unfriendly? No, he said, it would be 'not unacceptable' and even agreed to sign a written statement to this effect, though he insisted that it should also include his opinion that 'it would not lead to any results'.

Clearly, the statesmen of the warring nations would take no first step – indeed, would profess indifference –and doubtless it could have been a challenging task to bring political opinion in their own countries into agreement. But the women were not laughed out of court. The responses they received contain a curious note of what can only be called wistfulness. The warring leaders left the door a crack open, and there is sufficient evidence to suggest that, as human beings, they were yearning for someone else to open it wider. But, more than that, as statesmen, despite the reserve of their responses, they had, with only the one exception of France, dwelt on the inability of the nations at war to initiate any move to negotiation, and had indicated that they saw it as an important and expected role for the neutrals, almost an obligation.

Talking to the neutral nations

The second delegation, travelling to the neutral Scandinavian countries, included Emily Balch, Rosika Schwimmer, Chrystal Macmillan and Cor Ramondt-Hirschmann. Grace Wales went along at the beginning to lend a hand; although she did not attend the formal meetings with statesmen, she took the opportunity to talk to many peace activists in the Scandinavian countries and to diplomats in several embassies before returning to

Jane Addams photographed in 1915

Canada, and then to her job in Wisconsin. She remained active and would later take part in Henry Ford's peace initiative.

The delegation to the neutrals worked on and off throughout the summer and fall of 1915, sometimes all together, sometimes in pairs, sometimes joined by Aletta Jacobs. At times, individual enthusiasms and skills helped their work; at other times eagerness and over-confidence was a hindrance. The forceful character of Rosika Schwimmer, which played so essential a role in the launch of the whole initiative, rendered her increasingly unwilling to listen to wise advice, let alone accept a part in what most of the ICWPP women were trying, rightly, to set up as an efficient functioning democratic organisation with a responsible decision-making and reporting process. At this time the international Council of Women for Permanent Peace did not even have a constitution or an international office and its strength and leadership were effectively divided between Britain, The Netherlands and the United States.

Misunderstandings occurred, funds were hard to come by, occasionally opportunities were missed; those who cared about process were driven almost to despair. But none of this should take away from the picture of a remarkable enterprise, carried forward despite wartime difficulties of communication, dangers and hardships of travel, and some serious ill health. It also renders even more striking the willingness of individual statesmen to meet with them.

In the neutral nations the principles the women envoys stood for met with support among statesmen as well as in the general public. The Netherlands had a strong peace movement, and had, of course, hosted the Women's Congress, in the planning of which Aletta Jacobs had played a large part. Jacobs was not alone in hoping that Holland might be persuaded to take the lead in calling together a conference of neutral nations to offer a forum for mediation. Before leaving after the Congress, Addams had had a cordial meeting with the Dutch Prime Minister, Cort van der Linden, and she met with the Prime Minister again while the other Envoys were still travelling. He gave her active encouragement to find out informally from the American President, Woodrow Wilson, whether he would take part in a mediation initiative.

Public response was a factor in how the Envoys were met in every country that they visited, and must always have borne on how the statesmen received them. Almost everywhere, public meetings were organised, usually by local peace groups, and were well supported. In Switzerland, the leaders were more reserved in their response to the Envoys than elsewhere; Swiss statesmen, with some justification, feared

The Spokesman 139

the European war as a potential divisive element in their own nation, exacerbating tensions between their German-speaking and their French-speaking citizens. But even here, the Prime Minister said that his country would come in when other neutral nations made a move.

In Denmark the Envoys were well received; the reception by the leading statesmen was formal, and although there was no sign that they would take the lead, the Envoys thought that Denmark would join if the initiative came from elsewhere. In Norway, they met separately with the King, the Foreign Minister, and the Prime Minister, who all gave them considerable time and showed genuine interest in the proposals.

Wherever the envoys met with encouragement, they followed up. Schwimmer, with Chrystal Macmillan, made return visits to most of the northern neutral capitals before the summer of 1915 was over, bringing renewed hopes after they heard how the delegation to the war capitals had been received. Sweden and Holland were soon identified as the nations showing most promise. In Sweden, it became apparent during their meetings with Knut Wallenberg, the Foreign Minister, that he would like to see his country play a role in getting negotiations started, and would gladly host such a conference as that suggested in the plan brought forward by the Envoys. He had played an important part in keeping the Scandinavian nations from involvement in the war, and had earlier made his own attempt, on behalf of Sweden, to approach Germany with an offer of mediation. Understandably, he wanted to know that a conference of neutrals would not be 'unacceptable' to the belligerents (none would use the term 'welcome'), and he made use of the Envoys to sound them out on this issue. It was in response to his wish for evidence that they made a point of getting a signed note from Sazonov, in Russia. They were welcomed again by Wallenberg on their return from Russia and large, and enthusiastic public peace rallies suggested that he would have public support if he took action.

The Envoys continued to travel in hope after Jane Addams left Europe. Some of the reports touch on the vision of Jacobs that her country might emerge as a leader. Never mentioned but perceptible is the sense that perhaps Wallenberg or Cort van den Linden – in addition to their genuine desire to bring the slaughter to an end — might reach for the personal glory that would attend success.

A remarkable document drawn up by Rosika Schwimmer and Chrystal Macmillan, dated 2 August 1915, sums up their experiences and the responses they had met with, and spells out the way forward, emphasizing the need for a special method to meet the unprecedented difficulties of moving forward. The belligerents claimed that they could do nothing: '… only the neutrals can act in this matter. Every day's delay means loss, irreparable loss, not only to the belligerents but to the whole world. This method provides the machinery for taking the first steps towards a settlement. It is for the neutrals to put it into motion.'

A precise proposal follows: a group of five nations, Denmark, The Netherlands, Norway, Sweden and Switzerland should come together at the call of one (Sweden or Holland were identified as the most likely to take this initiative) and should then issue invitations to other neutral nations to form part of a conference, which would immediately begin, with the help of experts, to draw up preliminary proposals to submit to the warring nations. 'By this method of continuous mediation in which the proposals would be initiated by an impartial body we can hope to see established the peace based on the principles of freedom and justice for which all the belligerents in their official statements, whether to the public or to our delegations, declare themselves to be fighting.'

Overall, the European journeys of the envoys provided reason for hope. Approval and a tentative willingness to participate had come from the neutral nations, and leaders in the war nations had officially stated that they would not stand in the way. A scarcely concealed longing comes through the words of some individual statesmen.

Taking the message to Woodrow Wilson

Reservations expressed by European leaders, especially in countries supportive of the German side, about the extent to which the US could be seen as neutral, or indeed had any understanding of Europe, led Schwimmer and Macmillan to propose that the conference for continuous mediation should be convened by European neutrals. Nevertheless, they recognised the need for the United States to be included, and the neutral statesmen clearly saw that no serious official conference was likely to take place without US encouragement and participation. The Dutch Prime Minister, Cort van den Linden, spelled it out explicitly, saying that he could not take the initiative unless he knew that Wilson approved, and would bring the US into such a conference, telling the Envoys, 'If you can bring me as soon as possible unofficial[ly] a statement of Pres. Wilson's attitude I consider this as an act of great importance'.

Wilson had let it be known that he wanted to see Addams on her return from Europe, and she tried to recruit several well known British men known to be active for peace to accompany her, believing that a male presence would be helpful (according to Bertrand Russell this was because

Wilson was 'anti-feminist'). Russell met with her, and heard details of her visits in Europe. Initially he found Addams 'very impressive' and said that he would 'love' to go with her to see Wilson, although he feared that the British Embassy would be against it. But he was dissuaded, partly by circumstances but largely by meeting – less than a week later — with Alfred Jay Nock, a libertarian journalist then working for the American *Nation*. An acquaintance of William Jennings Bryan, Nock was a peace advocate, but wholly antagonistic to Jane Addams, whom he described to Russell as 'about as welcome [in Washington] as the black plague', a description accepted by Russell but hardly borne out by Wilson's keenness to meet with her.

President Wilson, in fact, was accessible to a degree hardly credible to our age, although at times he expressed reluctance to meet with delegates from belligerent nations. Over the next few months he met several times with Addams, Schwimmer and Balch, as well as a number of others supportive of intervention that might bring peace closer. Aletta Jacobs brought the President a direct, if informal, question from the Dutch Government repeating van den Linden's question as to whether he would like to take the lead in calling a conference of neutrals or, alternatively, would join such a conference if called by others. Some of Wilson's top-level advisers also met with one or other of the women and with others promoting the same cause of neutral facilitation of peace negotiations.

The efforts of the women envoys had not fallen on completely deaf ears in either belligerent or neutral nations. In a letter to House written in August 1915, Grey wrote of having been pressed by neutrals for a response to the formation of a conference of neutral states. He told House that such an effort could not be resented but that it had little chance of success unless the US took part. Significantly, although Grey spoke of Britain's current focus on victory, he did not dismiss the idea that the war might end by mediation, if the US facilitated the solution.

The women Envoys continued to press for a commitment and were joined by other influential US peace advocates, and by major peace societies. Dr David Starr Jordan, President of Stanford University, was deputed by a prestigious International Peace Congress held in San Francisco in October 1915 to meet with Wilson and ask him to convene a conference of neutrals. Advocates met with Wilson through November; some came away hopeful, others were discouraged, suggesting that he was indeed having trouble making up his mind.

Balch had understood in August that President Wilson 'said definitely that he would not wait to be asked to mediate, if he saw any opportunity to be of any use he would take it'. But the President's closest advisers, Colonel House and Robert Lansing, were firm if covert opponents of the scheme and did much to discredit it with Wilson; their influence far outweighed that of William Jennings Bryan, Secretary of State at the time. In July, House, notifying Wilson of a coming visit from Addams, had dismissed the journeys of the Envoys in a few contemptuous words: 'Jane Addams,' he wrote 'has accumulated a wonderful lot of misinformation in Europe. She saw von Jagow, Grey, and many others, and, for one reason or another, they were not quite candid with her, so she has a totally wrong impression.' Wilson, I think, had glimpsed the potential opportunity offered by the work of the women Envoys: House was quite unable to understand that what they had done was something that could only have been done by women in that strange period when they still lacked political power. In the long run, Wilson failed to take any initiative, or to give the needed leadership.

By November, it was often House who met with any who came to advocate for mediation; he seems to have developed skill in appearing to listen while having a closed mind, and even delighted in setting them to argue among themselves when he could. House undoubtedly would have liked to see the US play a stellar role in bringing the war to an end by diplomacy, but the plan he was himself developing, not revealed until some years later, depended more on playing the belligerents off against one another than it did on focusing on what of common ground there might be in the declared goals of the two sides, and seeking a point where mediation might begin.

Meanwhile time and events moved on, deaths demanded more deaths and the window of opportunity was closing. As the US advocates of peace came to realise that the President was not going to act, they explored the possibility and potential of a standing international conference of influential and respected private individuals, to perform the role that had been proposed for the neutral statesmen. Henry Ford, replete with money and more good will than good sense, hired a ship and set out for Europe with a motley assortment of peace people including some of the women who had been among the envoys. The journeys of the women envoys and what fruits they had borne had been the product of hard-won self discipline and team work, at times seriously flawed but never completely broken. The Ford Peace project, despite the good intentions and ability of many of those who set sail in the *Oscar II,* had no such framework, and was beset with lack of focus and interpersonal disagreements; we shall not follow that story here.

Once the USA entered as a belligerent, in 1917, any possible role as a mediator was of course at an end. There is plenty of evidence that Wilson listened to the women attentively; ironically, his famous 'Fourteen Points', brought to the Versailles table after victory, were largely based on the resolutions passed by the women of the Hague Congress: by then these principles of peace lacked the power they might have borne when there was a peace to be negotiated, not merely the spoils of victory to be debated.

Conclusion

I find enough evidence in the story of the journeys and of the reception accorded to the women envoys to suggest that, if only they had found one statesman great enough – preferably Woodrow Wilson — to take the ball and run with it, drawing others along with him, tentative peace negotiations might have opened before the end of 1915. Presented with a clear plan and strong presidential leadership, public opinion might well have rallied behind a vision of the United States as a peacemaker.

What this could have meant should not be measured only, or indeed mainly, in terms of the countless deaths that we know occurred during the next three years, but in the different spirit that might have informed the peace that followed. Imagine a world in which the Second World War had not happened.

***

In writing this article, I have used and briefly quoted from the following books:

Mercedes Randall: *Improper Bostonian*: *Emily Greene Balch* (N.Y.: Twayne, 1964); Addams, Balch and Hamilton: *Women at The Hague*, (1915, Garland reprint, 1972); Anne Wiltsher: *Most Dangerous Women* (London: Pandora, 1985); Mary Jean Woodard Bean: *Julia Grace Wales: Canada's Forgotten Heroine and the Quest for Peace* (Borealis Press, 2005); Sybil Oldfield, *Spinsters of this Parish* (London:Virago, 1984).

Other details and quotations are drawn from contemporary pieces, many handwritten, scattered through collections in the United States, Europe and the UK, from correspondence and reported conversations, notes made by several women who were present at an informal gathering in London, reports to their organization filed by delegates, and other personal recollections. I have drawn this material from the following collections: Catherine Marshall Papers, Cumbria Record Office; Internationaal Archief voor de Vrouwenbeweging, Amsterdam; Lady Ottoline Morrell Papers at

Humanities Research Center, University of Texas; several sub-collections in the Swarthmore College Peace Collection; Women's International League Papers at University of Colorado, Boulder. I appreciate the help I received from the archivists at these collections. At the time of my research, I was not able to obtain access to the Schwimmer/Lloyd Collection at the New York Public Library, but have made use of papers selected and sent to me by Edith Wynner.

I also appreciate permission to quote from Mary Sheepshanks, 'Women Suffrage and Pacifism', unpublished autobiography, seen by courtesy of Sybil Oldfield.

Detailed references can be supplied on request.

• •

 **WOMEN'S INTERNATIONAL LEAGUE FOR PEACE & FREEDOM**

The Women's International League for Peace and Freedom (WILPF) is an international non-governmental organisation (NGO) with National Sections covering every continent, an International Secretariat based in Geneva, and a New York office focused on the work of the United Nations (UN).

Since our establishment in 1915, we have brought together women from around the world who are united in working for peace by non-violent means and promoting political, economic and social justice for all.

Our approach is always non-violent, and we use existing international legal and political frameworks to achieve fundamental change in the way states conceptualise and address issues of gender, militarism, peace and security.

Our strength lies in our ability to link the international and local levels. We are very proud to be one of the first organisations to gain consultative status (category B) with the United Nations, and the only women's anti-war organisation so recognised.

Visit https://wilpf.org/ for more information

Airbrushed from history?

A Note on RSSF & May 68

Ruth Watson & Greg Anscombe

As the May 68 media and nostalgia machines got under way, occasional references were made to the UK's student revolt and its organisation RSSF, the Revolutionary Socialist Students Federation. This Note draws together a varied assortment of sources to assess what is known about what happened, suggesting that the British student rebellion of the 1968 period has largely been airbrushed out of modern history as ephemeral and implicitly a minor British copy-cat phenomenon in comparison to French, German and Italian and other European movements, and, of course, the various movements in the Unite States.

The impressive scale of recent student support for the campaign against the reduction of comprehensive pensions for university teachers is a reminder that, as a body, students have had, and can have a distinct role in progressive politics, nothwithstanding the careerism and elitism which has characterised official National Union of Student (NUS) associated politics at various — too many — periods.

Remember the long marches

Mature reflections after 50 years have their value, but one thematic ingredient, if not an actual material outcome — a piece of real history making — must be the long marches through the institutions taken by many from that generation of students. While there are many who have travelled outside the red lines of left activism and socialism, it is arguable that the collective march has sustained and enriched subsequent political life. It was, in this sense, not just student ferment and unrest: it was a rebellion, with honourable echoes in history and notable advances of ideology. In the UK, as elsewhere but not everywhere and in different ways, mainstream student politics through student unions and guilds was challenged by the Radical Student Alliance movement which rapidly transformed into the RSSF formation, conceived before May 68 if not to plot revolution, surely to demonstrate the case for a politics beyond reformism. That the French events got very close to triggering an actual French revolution defines differences of reality and circumstance, but not aspiration. For Britain, it gave a new politics which was already emerging in student circles a much wider meaning and deeper register.

A definitive identity?

As far as RSSF is concerned, basic references are meagre and elementary facts are misleadingly definite — the real first conference date was not at London's Roundhouse in November 68, though this has been referred to as 'founding' because a manifesto and organisational format was agreed. The start was in June 68 at LSE, after an initial proposal from a Leicester University occupation prior to France's May 68. The dating contributes to the quite false view that it was all very short-lived, had no pre-history and little outcome. Leadership matters are equally misrepresented: there was no relevance or role for the Jack Straws of this world. His opportunistic careerism dates from his overt rejection of student rebellion at the time, and his astute challenge to the mainstream NUS leaders in the name of, well, Jack the Lad, slithering icon of future generations of New Labour careerism. Other figures such as Tariq Ali played notable roles in opposing the Vietnam War, and supporting New Left politics, but were hardly involved in student politics, activism and events under the RSSF umbrella. Sectarian and formal political parties were involved, but they tailed the independents, and rejected the independents' thinking which was, roughly speaking, newly presented European marxisms and liberationist doctrines. They also tailed the associated formations. Not the least were the Schools Action Union (SAU), the Gay Liberation Front, many feminist formations, and pre professional groups such as ARSE (revolutionary architectural students), trainee teacher groups, theatre groups (AGITPROP), Cinema Action, art college groups and scientists, psychologists and philosophers in the making. Issues provoking occupations, sit-ins, lock-outs, marches and demonstrations, conferences and publications and manifestos filled the whole spectrum of anti capitalist and anti imperialist politics, and there was involvement in the Irish troubles.

Worker, trade union and labour movement connections were sought and gelled in ways quite different to the traditional politics of either, significantly, the official Communist Party or the lesser sectarian and *ouvrierist* groups. On the other hand, photos of official trade union marches with Gay Liberation Front banners — and others — just behind the front row reflected a commonality of political spirit if not lifestyle.

Even where books and authors cite official state records (see below) and provide extensive reading lists, there is no sense of primary historical fact. Indices to otherwise useful general books omit RSSF, show no evidence of seeking obvious sources such as local papers and university archives, which would show a very different picture.

The poverty of literature

This is especially true of the post 68 literature. Maybe its poverty reflects hard political facts and experience: because the rebellion and activism was so extensive and such an overt political break, well beyond the scale and character of 'the usual suspects of the lefty sects', many people did not want to self-publicize. The culture was essentially collective, impersonal, free in form but politically coherent and purposive. Fear was a big factor: victimisation by a UK state whose fundamental attitude was angry, repressive and punitive was much more extensive as a sanction than appeared from the celebrity episodes. Collective personality, anonymous work and non-iconic leadership were the dominant cultural style, to an extent necessarily so.

History deserves to be and can be better served: in contrast, for May 68 the French state has contributed a substantial and significant archival exhibition, alongside the predictable and proper history and politics reviews and debates (see below). Their exhibition opens the French state archives and treats the era as a contestation of power: the UK movement needs its own characterisation, but at a minimum it must include a major, if not the major and first serious challenge to the intellectual and cultural authority of the universities and Higher Education (HE) sector as bulwarks and foundations of UK state hegemony. Today's long accumulated subjection of higher education to neo-liberal dictates might be seen as the long tail of punishment for the 68 rebellion.

Edward Short's 'perps' ...

The UK Establishment's typically many-sided modus/animus was expressed most clearly by Secretary of State for Education, Edward Short. In January 69 he let fly:

'LSE has about 3,000 students. The disruptions that have taken place involve probably about 300 of these, though the real perpetrators are a tiny handful of people — fewer than half of one per cent . Of these, at least four are from the United States. These gentlemen are clearly not here to study, but to disrupt and undermine British institutions. They are the thugs of the academic world.'

RSSF's poster replied to Short showing a Tintin-style figure looking at an amazingly huge growing red mushroom with the counter view, graffiteed with 'only 1/2 of 1 per cent' and 'The revolution that is beginning will call into question not only capitalist society but industrial society. Social alienation must vanish from history. Imagination is seizing power.'

VCs — not medals, just ruthless repression

Vice Chancellors quickly got themselves organised, meeting first at Downing College Cambridge. Their correspondence and plans for victimisation/repression were discovered by Warwick students and widely circulated. Historian Edward Thompson, of Warwick University, subsequently edited the papers as *Warwick University Ltd*, published by Penguin in 1970 and reprinted by The Russell Press for Spokesman in 2014. The pitch of the VCs is hard to credit: a 26 'Principles of Treatment' document about handling student occupations from the Vice Chancellor of Bristol University talks of direct access to the Chief Constable in case of riot, police escort for tours of inspection, locking out teaching staff (in case of collusion?), solicitors to be instructed for injunctions and possible collective legal action, not just individual victimisation, bring in 'agents on particular aspects', 'harassing occupants by cutting off essential services', and the general aim that 'a weapon may be forged ... to give speedy redress to ... this technique of "direct acton".' Is comment needed?

A *cri de coeur* from LSE Secretary Harry Kidd, *The Trouble at LSE*, remains a fascinating case study of perplexed traditional authority and authoritarianism, published in 1969 by Oxford University Press and obviously written very quickly. A photo of police carrying — evicting — a student from LSE's Connaught House has the revealing caption 'The clearance of Connaught House'.

A velvet glove too ...

The velvet glove came from the extensive official and institutional work of the Parliamentary Select Committee (see below) advising local authorities not to summarily [sic] cut off student grants while probing the challenges facing student representatives within the NUS structures but avoiding ideological engagement. Its conclusion perhaps explains the story line of much later history: UK student rebellion not as bad as elsewhere, can be played down but containment needed. It runs to a main report and seven volumes of evidence, concluding that 'disrupters' are a tiny minority, but their support could not be ignored, that unrest had some legitimate causes which could be taken on board in reform, but that the legal powers of the para-state, i.e. publically funded higher education, needed clarification of its ultimate powers to command deference and compliance. The problem was legal authority apparently versus, but to be balanced with, free speech and legitimate critical capacity. Anyone familiar with the discourses of the UK governing class would see the signals and read the codes: and note, wisely, that there is not a drop of recognition that the classic ideologies of politics had any presence other than as 'disrupters'.

Heady words then, on both sides, but they reflect a sense of substantial and significant events, political challenge and change, and genuine threat to the established order. That deserves serious historical analysis, not least because this resistance and rebellion needs to join in the ranks of the other version of UK state history, which reveals routine, successive and deep challenges to a political hegemony. But one big political outcome can be asserted with some certainty: the aftermath, in later life and through family and community and political heritage, saw the Blair/Brown Iraq War sycophancy challenged by almost two million people on the streets. Nearly two million, not the tens of thousands who characterised anti-Vietnam war demonstrations in the 60s, when the student rebellion helped to keep up the pressure on Wilson's government to stay clear of US war-making in Vietnam. There were many ideological and political culture outcomes, too: they deserve more than casual judgements.

A surprisingly limited field

The 50th anniversary has seen only the one substantial work in the UK by Richard Vinen, London University history professor, *The Long 68 — Radical Protest and its Enemies* (see below). It has had good reviews but has no forensic reach into the UK situation. The *London Review of Books* has run a commendable interview with Tariq Ali, valuable about his role and oversight capacities, but not based on direct student movement experience as such. There is also the republishing by Verso of the quite separate and important texts of the *May Day Manifesto 1968* programme of analysis associated with Raymond Williams. Given the role and contribution of then *New Left Review* associates to the UK 68 universities revolt, it is disappointing that NLR has not claimed any heritage. Many historical studies of sixties and seventies Britain — more correctly, Britain and Ireland since Ireland north and south was involved — are overwhelmingly dependent on secondary sources. An American study of 2012, *British Student Activism in the Long Sixties* (see below), is astutely flagged on Google as a 'welcome addition to a surprisingly limited field'.

Thematic worker/student control issues

The Bertrand Russell Peace Foundation is to be thanked for publishing this Note. Its own initiative to re-activate workers' control politics occurred in the same period. The Institute for Workers' Control's politics, too, were independent, about self-organisation, producer communities, and challenging the power of established authorities across a wide agenda. After several years of preparation, the IWC was founded in March 1968 at a conference in Nottingham, which contained and sustained student workshops. *Students at Hull* by Alistair Kee was the first BRPF 'Paper on Democracy in Higher Education'. Of course, the Russell Foundation itself was in part shaped by one of the big commonalities of 68 — the Vietnam War, including active association with the Vietnam Solidarity Campaign (VSC), although the Foundation was established a few years earlier, when it could be argued the ferment was starting to emerge. From 1966 onwards, there had been actions, charters, calls for university reform — the French events gave them a new authority and resonance.

This Note seeks to put on record some elementary RSSF data, to assist readers and maybe stimulate memories. It has been compiled from a variety of sources and views.

* * *

Revolutionary Socialist Students Federation

Politics and Organisation

RSSF's Formation and development

The need for a coordinating organisation was raised at a Leicester University meeting in late Spring term 1968 after the Leicester occupation/sit-in, with LSE and Essex representatives and some support from International Socialist activists for an 'independent' student organisation initiative. This would advance on the recently formed Radical Student Alliance, the key player in the LSE events, which started in 1966. A Free University event at Essex University in 1967 might be regarded as a prime mover, but LSE's anti capitalist and anti imperialist programme started earlier, in 1966. Leicester claims the first occupation/sit-in, while the last recorded occupation was Liverpool.

A full preparatory conference was proposed at a two-day LSE conference in June 68, after the French May events. This founding conference agreed a manifesto and the organisational format of a loose federation of individuals and groups with red bases. It took place at The Roundhouse, London, 8/9 November 1968. A co-ordination bureau was set up at 59 Fleet Street, and National Coordination Committee meetings commenced, held at various sites. More than a thousand individual members registered, and over 100 institutions — including colleges of all varieties, schools and political groups — were represented. There were 72 RSSF base groups routinely involved, 29 in the London area, 10 in

Scotland, three in Wales, and one in Northern Ireland. The Second National Conference was at Manchester University in March 69, the third at Imperial College London in December 69, after a Leicester Summer Seminar. The last conference was in Liverpool in April 1970. Many sectarian groups, most notably IS, withdrew support from the Imperial Conference onwards, in response to the independents' emerging aim of establishing an ongoing cadre network. (See below for Study Group Report 'Political Theory of the Student Movement'.)

RSSF Actions

These took many forms, most commonly involving occupations and sit-ins and teach-ins, marches and free style demonstrations, connecting to community and issue actions such as the property speculation underpinning the emerging housing crisis. The squat at No 9 Piccadilly, London, saw a schoolgirl arrested as the ringleader. RSSF organised a solidarity contingent with the Northern Irish Civil Rights Association (NICRA) to march from Belfast to Dublin at Easter 1969 for civil rights north and south, much of the organising being down to the recently formed People's Democracy movement. It needs to be remembered that while LSE had sit-ins and teach-ins, it also had a lock-out, reinforced by new steel gates and police horses, and its staff and student representatives were victimised, as were many others at different institutions, while heavy fines and prison sentences were imposed elsewhere. At LSE, the governors' application for court injunctions, sanctioned by gaol sentences for 'disrupters', was rejected by the courts. A common demand in sit-ins and occupations was for fair and open student disciplinary codes and processes; struggles were underpinned by help from legal professionals, and tribute is due to London University's Professor John Griffiths, culminating in his defence of the expelled students at the last major sit-in at Liverpool University.

Violence from the police on demonstrations was always present as a threat, and *agent provocateurs* were uncovered; these measures were justified by public allegations of student violence from politicians, vice chancellors and the media. In contrast, the action of the 'opening' the steel gates at LSE, and some locks on doors of squatted/occupied college property, was minor and mild: later, the similarly mild Garden House Hotel protest in Cambridge was used as an excuse for gaol sentences, maybe partial retribution for earlier embarrassments caused by a different student generation over the disrupted visit of Henry Brook, the UK's last hanging Home Secretary, in 1963. The Garden House demonstration was against a junket dinner for visiting Greek big-wigs representing the military junta. The Liverpool University occupation ended with expulsions and a legal counter-challenge, constituting a virtual trial, but without jury or public gallery.

On a less solemn note, some occupations ended with cleaner premises than they started. At Guildford College of Art an occupation about student treatment and representation was planned to be ended with security staff brought in to evict students. Four of the security staff, when they understood the situation, crossed sides and joined the students.

A year of occupations

Academic studies suggest there were nine major occupations during 1968: Keele, Edinburgh, Bristol, York, Leeds, Leicester, Oxford and Cambridge, and Hornsey and Guildford Art Colleges. These are recorded by S Webster (2015) 'Protest Activity in the British Student Movement 1945-2011', a PhD study (see below). *New Left Review's* Ronald Fraser (see below) has another chronology, and a useful international concordance, while a hostile but interesting treatment by Margaret Anne Rooke (see below), written just after the 68 period, as was Fraser's, has considerable and detailed reportage. This book makes reference to events and issues at 92 institutions of higher education.

A solidarity leaflet (with LSE) after the Round House conference records another scale of activity, with students at 22 colleges of various kinds expressing active solidarity with the LSE students in occupations, mass meetings, teach-ins, donations and declarations.

Political formations and ideologies

While opposition to racism and colonial/imperial university links was an early and continuing theme, the agenda of issues was amazingly diverse, providing triggers for protest and action and continuous debate. But vindictiveness about student bids for participation, transparency, influence and democracy — abbreviated to 'student power' by university and higher education authorities — transposed a broader ferment of ideas into struggles and contestation. Disappointment with the Wilson Government, the start of higher education policy viewing students as higher grade market labour under traineeship, and cultural changes — the Stones, Beatles and Hendrix had campus support and were provided venues — and other well documented openings, led many in the university establishments to see their privileges and demands for deference and compliance under profound threat. Traditional student socialists had seen their Labour Party student organisation, NALSO, closed down in 1966. So much was happening before the French May 68 events, and other international struggles gave a global and systemic meaning to issues which in themselves could look less momentous. Personal lifestyle, curriculum, the right to free speech, and active political life as opposed to allegedly privileged and deferential apprenticeship were the ingredients of a movement deeply rooted and widely resonant. It contrasted sharply in style, aspiration and scale with the practices of traditional sectarian groupings, their mechanical marxisms, *ouvrierisms* and revolutionary rhetorics, although they were strongly present in many areas and, as individuals, often played important roles. The independents — the keyword for practical RSSF politics — outnumbered the sectarian Trotskysists, of two main varieties, the Maoists, and mingled most easily with liberationist groupuscules. In a separable category, orthodox communists found their party cool and patrician, wanting debate and policy talks, not actions. It was culturally uncomfortable with new modalities of feminism, gay liberation and militant activism, but its individual student cadres were good RSSFers and brought leadership and political skills. RSSF's base politics was distinctly independent, and in open debate about actions, both starting and ending, it rallied the decisive majorities.

European marxism's revival coalesced with American anti-racism and liberationisms and, quite soon, a new politics of power assertion turning into revolutionary challenge. This was reflected in student, ethnic group struggles and, in the United States, in organised working class industrial life. Black independent union movements were formed in the major car companies (DRUM, FRUM) around Detroit and the COBAS (committees of the Base) emerged in Italy. France's militant CGT led and won concrete gains as well as demonstrating its fundamental class politics. Britain's traditional marxists were of some variety and rather varied traction. Their *ouvrierist* /worker orientation had an arguably self-defeating result. When they withdrew from RSSF and the new student movement, they cut themselves off from a wide audience, and an ongoing and systemic area of struggle, which, as higher education subsequently showed, has played a major role in subsequent national politics. Had that not happened, the long marchers might have been more numerous.

Communications

A plethora of magazines, reports, political texts and posters appeared, many directly as RSSF. Poster workshops used self-made silk-screen technique, while duplicated and offset litho publications flourished with the occasional wall newspapers. Student papers abounded, formal ones from student guilds, and others newly created. The Cambridge 1/- (Shilling) Paper started the now established idea of a student critique of universities, a kind of insiders university WHICH, while national independent political media took off (*Black Dwarf, Time Out, Oz,* etc). American, French, Italian and German student movement publications and new Marxist literature were in free and frequent circulation. A national newsletter was produced by RRSF's off-campus bureau at 59 Fleet Street, round the corner from LSE. Offset litho printing had just become available, allowing bigger distributions and quicker production. Otherwise, Roneos and Gestetners did the work, especially after the new photocopy machines were removed from free access.

Leadership

There were no Cohn Bendits, and no Rudi Dutschkes — the German student (SDS) leader shot by anti-communist Josef Bachmann, resulting in premature death. The two student official leaders and two lecturers sacked at LSE became what would now be termed 'icons', but of victimisation, not leadership, which was firmly rooted in mass assemblies and collective initiatives. Documents were often signed pseudonymously, or contributory names listed to signal collective production and commitment. Victimisation was, however, frequent, fervent and random, revealing the hysteria of the university authorities and their inability to understand the political models and processes of the student movement.

RSSF co-ordinated events

The LSE 'Open the Gates' march was organised under RSSF auspices, mounting a national solidarity demonstration of towards 20,000, a symbolic political high point being a covert route plan which countermanded a police ban on marching past both the US Embassy and the South African Embassy on the way to LSE. Here, serried police horses barred the narrow entrance street. The Belfast to Dublin march, with mass arrests at Newry, supported the 'Civil Rights North & South' movement associated with PD (People's Democracy) and NICRA (Northern Ireland Civil Rights Association).

Long marches of students, ideologies and politics: five currents?

Five currents were activated, embedded and constituted in subsequent political history by the UK student movement, most of them, of course, internationally resonant, but some particularly characteristic of UK governance and state power. Strategic doctrine number one was the long march through the institutions: occupations started did not just fizzle out, but asserted re-entry terms as dominant issues.

Second was the political imperative of base organisation and open democracy. Instead of electoral arithmetic, community voice and authority and street numbers became a norm, outside the two (and two-and-a-half party system). This was maybe re-established, as much as being new; the newness being the student constituency.

Third was basic disengagement from establishment political norms and, hence, established modes of conflict resolution, mediation and compromise and the prescribed return to 'normality' after bouts of 'unrest' — the Select Committee terminology. This involved the idea that parliamentary democracy needed to work for the people below, not those above, through principled engagement and the pursuit of traction and outcomes for popular social issues.

Fourthly, that processes of democratic participation and constitutional control were not only fundamental but could be made to work and 'prove' a different way of running society. With higher education in the frame, this was both possible and necessary. The language of exposition and articulation for this 'control/power' politics came, most obviously, from socialism's workers' control traditions and deeper doctrines of producer rights, wherever they operated in economy and society.

Fifth came ideological affiliation: this may be portrayed, for simplicity's sake, as an independent marxism and liberationism. This often appeared as new utopias, but equally could be sharply focused: schoolchildren in Berlin broke away from a demonstration protesting about the Soviet invasion of Czechoslovakia, occupied an auditorium and debated the issues, teaching their student and parental generations — and the public — that the really relevant, true demand had to be 'Russians out of Prague, Americans out of Berlin'. RSSF's support for civil rights north and south in Ireland might be seen as a minor example of a similar political capability in the face of frozen, check-mated global and local politics.

These currents, tenets and approaches constituting perhaps a political ideology in its own right, motivated, explained and energised political action. Seen most powerfully, once uncovered and made available, in the long development of western marxisms on the one hand and feminism and gender rights on another, they de-passed the transatlantic consensus version of deep political truth and history as freedom, humanism and democracy versus collectivism. Overall, the long march of ideologies after 68, having found a market place for effect and traction, was as much of a historical product as the long march of actual people from 1968.

Literature

RSSF Manifesto: adopted at London's Roundhouse conference, November 68.

RSSF Red Texts 1 and RSSF Red Texts 2: RT1 has accounts of the June 68 LSE founding conference of RRSF and base reports. RT2 contained a range of papers including anti Nazi league campaigning, features on housing, architecture and squatting, and one of many circulating marxist bibilographies.

RSSF Irish Paper: for the NICRA Belfast-Dublin march, May 69 (8 pages)

RSSF Political Theory of the Student Movement — Notes for a Marxist Critique, March 1971, a substantial and marketed report, containing a chronology, review of formally declared political tendencies in RSSF, political analysis of RSSF politics, and a theory reading list. Commissioned by RSSF conference April 70.

Newssheets, magazines, reports, wall posters and posters

References have been found to the following publications: **Before the Barricades,** Essex RSSF magazine, with cover of France, schools students' issues, and the RSSF manifesto. **The Cambridge Shilling Paper** ran for a good period. **Subversity** was produced at Sheffield University. **Incite** was by York RSSF. **Sublation** was a theoretical magazine from Leicester and **Cadre** came from Leicester RSSF. Birmingham's Student Guild paper **Redbrick** played a strong role, as did many other 'official' student papers. **The Mole** came from Brighton, **Red Notes** from London University Union, Gower St. **The Dossier** came from Manchester University, **Before the Barricades** from Essex University RSSF, and **Open Conspiracy** from Bristol University.

Vanguard newspaper came from the Schools Action Union. **Paper Tiger** was produced by the Birmingham 491 Group. **Praxis** came from Bradford University RSSF. **Cardiff People's Paper** was, like others, community based. **The Eysenck Paper** was produced by trainee teachers at Bingley Teacher Training College. **SCUM** came from City of London College, **Hull Left** reflected a broad politics, and **The Red Flag** came from Chelsea Art College.

Contemporary accounts

LSE: The Natives are Restless, Paul Hoch & Vic Schoenbach, Sheed & Ward (left catholic publishers) 1969

Student Power, Penguin Special, with New Left Review, 1969, edited Alex Cockburn & Robin Blackburn, a broad based collection

House of Commons Select Committee on Education & Science, Report and seven volumes of evidence, July 1969

The Political Theory of the Student Movement, March 1971, postscript to a 100-page analysis by an RSSF study group.

1968: A Student Generation in Revolt, Ronald Fraser, Chatto & Windus. By a New Left Review editorial board member and oral historian, authoritative on the global movement but light coverage of situation in Britain.

Anarchy & Apathy: Student Unrest 1968-1970, Margaret Anne Rooke, Hamish Hamilton, 1971. Most indexed for RSSF, a rightwing *cri de coeur* for the established order but an interesting account.

50th Anniversary & other accounts

Richard Vinen, *The Long 68: Radical Protest and its Enemies*, Allen Lane, 2018. This manages two paragraphs around RSSF and left groups. Otherwise useful, with some state archival sources but essentially a political interpretation reflecting more about post-millennial times than the actualities of 68.

68 — Les Archives du Pouvoir: French National Archives, two exhibitions and online catalogue, Paris *www.archives-nationales.culture.gouv.fr*

PhD thesis: S. Webster, Manchester University, 2015. Nine occupations recorded in 1968 in 'Protest Activity in the British Student Movement 1945-2011', a study focused on Manchester University and LSE.

Days in the Life, Jonathan Green, Voices from the English Undergound 1961-71, Minerva, 1988

1968 The Year That Rocked the World, Mark Kurlansky, Jonathan Cape, 2004. Very little about the UK, politically not unlike Vinen but without new sources.

Background

Herbert Marcuse's works, notably 'One Dimensional Man' and other formative politics provided the basis for the seminal 'Dialectics of Liberation Conference' held in London at the Roundhouse in July 1967. Published by Pelican in 1968, edited by David Cooper, it contains a useful Marcuse text and several invaluable papers.

Reflections on the Revolution in France: 1968, Pelican, published 1970, edited by Charlie Posner, is a model of contemporary document and analysis.

French Revolution 1968, a Penguin Special by Patrick Seale and Maureen McConville, published rapidly in 1968, is a professional journalists' eyewitness account of considerable value.

New Left Review No 52, Nov-Dec 68, is a celebratory special issue analysis of the French events, including a Lenin text on the Russian student movement and an interesting introductory essay.

The Student Revolt, one of two books published by Panther in 1968, contains speeches and documents from the Paris activists.

The Beginning of the End, Panther 1968, contains two long analytical essays by Tom Nairn of *New Left Review* and Angelo Quattrocchi, Paris journalist working for the Italian journal *Avanti*. Nairn taught at Hornsey College of Art, London, and Quattrocchi was an eyewitness to the Paris events.

Imagination in Power: The occupation of factories in France in 1968 by Andrée Hoyles, published by Spokesman Books, Nottingham, in 1973.

How and Why Industry Must Be Democratised

Edited by
Ken Coates & Wyn Williams

A full report on the 1968 Workers' Control Conference together with all Conference Papers

THE INSTITUTE FOR WORKERS' CONTROL

OTTOLINE

Ottoline Morrell died 80 years ago, in April 1938, and lies buried in North Nottinghamshire. Some 23 years earlier, in April 1915, Bertrand Russell had treated her to a visit to nearby Bolsover Castle, her favourite haunt. There, as she recalls in her Memoirs, she quoted Bertie an 'old ballad' about Welbeck Abbey, Hardwick Hall, Bolsover Castle and Worksop Manor, written in the 1620s by a Dr Andrewes.

Hardwicke for hugeness, Worsope for height,
Welbecke for use, and Bolser for sighte;
Worsope for walks, Hardwicke for hall,
Welbecke for brewhouse, Bolser for all.
Welbecke a parish, Hardwicke a court,
Worsope a pallas, Bolser a fort;
Bolser to feast, Welbecke to ride in,
Hardwicke to thrive, and Worsope to bide in.
Hardwicke good house, Welbecke good keepinge,
Worsope good walks, Bolser good sleepinge;
Bolser new built, Welbecke well mended,
Hardwicke concealed, and Worsope extended.
Bolser is morn, Welbecke day bright,
Hardwicke high noone, Worsope good night;
Hardwicke is now, and Welbecke will last,
Bolser will be, and Worsope is past.
Welbecke a wife, Bolser a maide,
Hardwicke a matron, Worsope decaide;
Worsope is wise, Welbecke is wittie,
Hardwicke is hard, Bolser is prettie.
Hardwicke is rich, Welbecke is fine,
Worsope is statelie, Bolser divine;
Hardwicke a chest, Welbecke a saddle,
Worsope a throne, Bolser a cradle.
Hardwicke resembles Hampton court much,
And Worsope Windsor, Bolser Nonesuch;
Worsope a duke, Hardwicke an earl,
Welbecke a viscount, Bolser a pearl.
The rest are jewels of the sheere,
Bolser the pendant of the eare.

Exploring
Nottinghamshire
Writers

Rowena Edlin-White

A working-class hero is something to be

Ross Bradshaw

Nottingham's good fortune was to attract a wandering bookseller, who recounts his take on the literary hinterland of the old Coalfield. In 2018, Five Leaves Bookshop became Independent Bookshop of the Year.

Class is that big thing we don't talk about in relation to fiction. Mostly we don't talk about it at all.

At the start of D.H. Lawrence's *The Rainbow*, he describes the pastoral scene of men working the fields, in the shadow of the church tower, working good land in the way they had for generations. The men were stolid – 'inert' writes Lawrence – the women of the farms being more the go-getters. Creeping in were the railways, the mines, ugly industries for ugly people. People whose children the girl schoolteacher Ursula would beat to show them their place on her way out of her class – and, ironically, towards feminism, socialism, lesbianism, and education.

Once, at the D.H. Lawrence Birthplace Museum in Eastwood, I heard a former miner berating Lawrence because of his class. Not because Lawrence's mother was a bit above the position of a miner, but because Lawrence's father was an 'overman', the man who directed the work in the pit, the one who drove the pace. Such were the gradations within the class that a barely literate miner working in filth was seen as different by the men whose work he controlled.

It was Stanley Middleton – mentioned later – who taught me something else about class, and that was to do with religious observance. The working class went to chapel, the middle class to church. You can notice it if you look. In Lowdham there is one remaining Methodist chapel of the three that once operated in a village where textiles and railways were once important. They are in the village, the church is on the outskirts, the nearest house being what is still called Manor House, just across the road. D.H. Lawrence's early companion, Jessie Chambers, also remarks on this about her time with Lawrence when local aspirational families moved from chapel to church.

It is often assumed that when Arthur Seaton opens Alan Sillitoe's *Saturday Night and Sunday Morning* by falling drunk downstairs this was the start of the regional working class novel. Seaton was different. Someone recently reminded me of the opening scene of the Karel Reisz film where Seaton swaggers, runs for a bus. Nottingham was his city. Nobody could hold him back, not the bosses, not the unions, and not the women. He was in control. Though another reading of the book would put Seaton's Doreen winning the gender wars.

There is a progenitor to Arthur Seaton. *Penny Lace* by Hilda Lewis, published in 1946, has the Mr Penny of the title swaggering. Nothing could hold him back, not the bosses, not the unions, and not the women. And he took control by learning his trade – the trade of lace – and opening a mill in Long Eaton, out of reach of the lace trade unions so he could undercut the Nottingham firms and put his own former master out of business. I've often wondered if Sillitoe had read this book. Read the two books side by side so you can compare and contrast.

But it is coal that runs through the Nottingham working-class novel. Leslie Williamson, from Lawrence's Eastwood, in *Jobey* gave the rougher side of miners' lives – describing two miners solving their disagreement by kicking each other's shins with their pit boots on until one fell. On the other hand Stanley Middleton, in his best book, *Harris's Requiem*, described the packed-out concert of the Blidworth Band:

> 'The band all wore their military caps; we've paid for 'em, you shall see 'em. … There was none of that demanding concert-hall cough, no last minute titter. The music was starting and there was a money's worth to be got.'

The Band played a concert of Beethoven, *Finlandia*, and 'finally a mighty tone poem, specially composed with solos galore'. This was the cultured side of the mining community. Middleton mostly wrote about lower middle-class life, but he understood the class from which he came.

Mining. It is hard not to be moved by Lawrence's 'The Collier's Wife', a poem about a pit accident. Or the opening scene of the children's book *The Secret World of Polly Flint* by Helen Cresswell, which starts with Polly's father being brought up injured from the pit. Or the modern writer Deborah Tyler-Bennett describing the four lines devoted to her great-grandfather in the local paper, killed in a mining accident on Valentine's Day, 1914, while 'Fifty lines on how King George may visit/the Duke of Portland and attend the hunt/and thirty on a bride-to-be named Blisset/whose name on marriage will be Lady Blunt'. There were once 40,000 miners in Nottinghamshire, so it is hardly surprising there are so many literary references. But the Nottingham history of textiles – once employing 25,000 workers — is less represented, perhaps because most of those workers were women.

Tony Hill brings us almost to the end of the mining era with his autobiographical novel, *If the Kids are United*, writing about Jacksdale. The title comes from the Sham 69 song (but you knew that). His book is a roughly affectionate story of that former mining town, then in terminal decline thanks to Thatcherism. In his *The Palace and the Punks* Tony also described the life and times of The Grey Topper, an unlikely successful punk venue in his home town.

I'll move on from mining, and see what the women were saying, but in Nottinghamshire and other former mining areas it's hard to leave behind. I remember going to an NUM rally at the Usher Hall in Edinburgh, in the early seventies. Hearing the mining leaders Lawrence Daly quoting Shelley long before Jeremy Corbyn did ('Ye are many, they are few...') and Mick McGahey replying with Shakespeare ('The fault, dear Brutus, is not in our stars, But in ourselves, that we are underlings') did more to tell me of the importance of literature in working-class life than did my six years of secondary school.

Daly and McGahey were autodidacts. Older Nottingham readers will remember The Cosmo – the Cosmopolitan Debating Society. Its last years were painful, but it was once the arena for the sort of autodidacts, mostly men, who appeared in Sillitoe's novel *The Open Door* and Philip Callow's *The Hosanna Man*. One striking thing about Sillitoe's Nottingham novels is that, save for the occasional bohemian, the world outside the working class barely existed.

All I knew of Nottinghamshire writing before I came here was reading the dirty bits in D.H. Lawrence, which had no impact on me, when I was an immature teenager. Thankfully I was a bit more mature when I arrived in Nottingham, in 1978, to live in the building where the magazine *Peace News* was then produced. Over the road was a large semi-permanent graffito saying 'Socialism will come, riding on a bicycle'. My kind of town.

Another graffito, elsewhere, was also attractive in its own way – big letters on the Forest 'mmm ... marijuana'. Surprisingly, that was either a hangover or a reprise of the same graffito mentioned in Ray Gosling's *Personal Copy: a memoir of the Sixties*: the first book that gave me a sense of place in Nottingham. *Peace News* sat on the fringe of St Ann's, where Gosling had lived and campaigned against the destruction of the suburb made famous by Ken Coates and Bill Silburn's *Poverty: the Forgotten Englishmen* (still available from Spokesman Books). But rereading Gosling now it is his cameos of the City that strike me. Saturday afternoons at the Kardomah looking out over the City '"Just waiting for a friend," you'd say to the nippie.' Sundays down the Market Square, the Sally Bash at one end and the Communist John Peck on his stand at the other. Gosling describes how Arnold Wesker's *Centre 42*, a national touring project to bring culture to the trade unions, bit the dust in Nottingham with local promoters putting on competing events at the same time. There are lots of literary nuggets, Colin MacInnes, Philip Callow... and a visiting Adrian Henri, delighted to see a bus going to – or possibly called – Arnold.

The '60s was a decade of change for working-class people. Alan Fletcher, in his three self-published novels of Mod life, described himself and his colleagues as the first generation of working-class youth which had money in its pockets. Wanting to spend it on looking good. To get away from the dreariness of the demob suit and the flat cap.

Michael Standen, in *Start Somewhere* (republished by Shoestring Press) catches a moment when the previously sharp divisions in class are starting to fall apart. His novel describes a teenage romance. Mr Griffin – a grocer – warns his son:

'You be careful. Their station isn't ours. They have a different road of going on. Her father's someone in the Town Hall; I've seen his name in the *Post* ... If you think I'm complaining because you're mixing with a good class of person, I'm not. Miss Cooper's got real breeding ... So don't start treating her like the girls round here.'

Next thing, people will not be standing up when the Queen comes on at the cinema.

I mentioned women's voices. From the working class of that period, in Nottinghamshire, there aren't many who have come my way. That is not to say there are no books. The publisher Persephone has been busy rescuing Dorothy Whipple. Worth reading, but her books are those of the well-off, the people who had servants. What the servants had to say is not recorded.

A more dated writer yet is Rose Fyleman. I'll summarise one of her stories. A group of children (think Famous Five) come across a caravan, nearby was a baby in its cot, nobody else in sight. The obvious solution was that the baby had been stolen by Gypsies, 'because they do, you know', such an assumption being confirmed by the baby being blue-eyed and blond. So, some of the children rescue the baby while others head off to the road to stop any car with 'decent looking people' to get the police. Of course, the baby turns out not to be a stolen baby at all, but the nurse of a nice respectable couple, holidaying in their caravan, had left it out in the open (then to be stolen by those hideous, racist middle-class white children) while she went spooning with the boy in the farm next door.

A restorative read after that is Carol Lake – not Nottingham, but Derby. Lake has been overlooked of late, which is a shame, for she won *The Guardian* fiction award with *Rosehill*, set in our rival city. Her other book, *Switchboard Operators*, describes with gentle humour that now-vanished but once-important job from a woman's point of view.

Nicola Monaghan's first novel, *The Killing Jar*, was set among criminals on Nottingham's Bestwood estate she was brought up on, as was Derrick Buttress in an earlier generation, while Kim Slater's novel for older children, *Smart*, paints an ugly picture of the life for an autistic boy in The Meadows area of the city. Nicola remarked that her novel did not reflect the positive community spirit of her estate, but that it was easier to write a novel with crime at the heart rather than a feel-good novel about people being nice to one another.

But the face of our city, our county has changed over the last few years. On the Market Square you are likely to hear Polish, Romany, one of the Kurdish languages. Working-class Nottingham has changed again. So far Kevin Fegan has been the main writer to pick up on this. In *Let the Left Hand Sing* he walks down an imaginary street, knocking on doors, asking people to tell him their stories. There you will find, beside the Jamaican woman who remembers the Anansi stories of her childhood and the Ukrainian man who has lived in exile for fifty years, a woman from the Sudan 'who was eight when the soldiers came'. Kevin himself is a migrant, from an Irish family who came to the Midlands for want of work.

We do forget some of our past. If you've read it, can you remember the title of the first chapter of the book at the head of this article, *The Rainbow*? It's 'How Tom Brangwen Married a Polish Lady', the lady in question coming from a refugee family. We go in circles. But Nottingham does remember its working-class past – Christy Fearn writes about the Luddites, as does A.R. Dance with *Narrow Marsh,* which opens with a hanging.

Thus far there is no great Nottinghamshire call-centre novel, but the working class has not yet said its last word even if, in novels such as Phil

Whitaker's *The Face* and in so much of John Harvey's work, it is the streets of the city that give the books their Nottingham feel as much, perhaps more than, the people who walk them.

Ross Bradshaw contributed this essay to
Exploring Nottinghamshire Writers
by Rowena Edlin-white, Five Leaves Publications, £12.99
www.fiveleavesbookshop.co.uk

For man, the vast marvel is to be alive. For man, as for flower and beast and bird, the supreme triumph is to be most vividly, most perfectly alive. Whatever the unborn and the dead may know, they cannot know the beauty, the marvel of being alive in the flesh. The dead may look after the afterwards. But the magnificent here and now of life in the flesh is ours, and ours alone, and ours only for a time. We ought to dance with rapture that we should be alive and in the flesh, and part of the living, incarnate cosmos. I am part of the sun as my eye is part of me. That I am part of the earth my feet know perfectly, and my blood is part of the sea. My soul knows that I am part of the human race, my soul is an organic part of the great human soul, as my spirit is part of my nation. In my own very self, I am part of my family. There is nothing of me that is alone and absolute except my mind, and we shall find that the mind has no existence by itself, it is only the glitter of the sun on the surface of the waters.

Apocalypse, D H Lawrence

Reviews

Bolshevik

Steven A. Smith, *Russia in Revolution: An Empire in Crisis 1890-1928*, Oxford University Press, 272 pages, hardback ISBN 9780198734826, £25.00

Russia in Revolution was published to mark the centenary of the two revolutions of 1917, in February and October in the old Gregorian calendar, or March and November in the present-day Julian calendar. Whatever the date, the Bolshevik revolution was the first successful seizure of power by a Marxist party committed to implementing socialism. As the author makes abundantly clear, the problem for the Bolsheviks was that Russia was a latecomer to industrialisation. It was a relatively backward country whose economy was still dominated by agriculture and whose mass politics, even after the 1905 revolution and the establishment of the *Duma* or parliament, was still inchoate. Neither had Russia managed a 'bourgeois revolution', a factor repeatedly pointed out by Lenin's detractors within the Bolshevik party — that the proletarian revolution could not be successful and must defer to its bourgeois counterpart. For Lenin the horrors of World War One and the February revolution had changed everything, placing Russia at the head of a European wave of revolution. The Bolsheviks hoped that unrest in Germany had gained sufficient traction to alienate large sections of the working class, and that revolution was possible. This is, perhaps, an aspect of the Bolshevik strategic imperative to which Smith does not give enough weight. The Bolsheviks were united in their hope that Germany would come to the rescue of the fledgling Soviet state — they were to be sadly disappointed.

The book paints a comprehensive picture of Russian society prior to the 1905 and 1917 revolutions. Change was happening, but it was to prove too little too late. The working population was largely ill educated, and the Russian Empire was run by an indolent, repressive autocracy, which had at its head a remote narcissistic Tsar surrounded by a fawning court and the looming figure of Rasputin. (With the country in turmoil on the day the state Duma was to have its first session, Nicholas II wrote in his diary 'April 14th - Took a walk in a thin shirt and took up paddling again'.) The author paints a picture of a sclerotic society, order maintained by the secret police (the *Okhrana*), the army, the Cossacks, plus a harsh bureaucracy and an orthodox church wedded to the *status quo*. Together they ruled over a vast landmass with a multi-ethnic and multilingual population. Reforms were attempted, and civil society was developing a factory-owning bourgeoisie in urban areas. In the vast countryside some progressive landowners participated in local government through the *zemstvo* — but all were loath to challenge the autocracy. In 1914, if Russia was backward industrially, by the end of the World War One and the Civil War the situation was infinitely worse. Smith describes the situation in these stark words, 'The collapse of industry together with grave food shortages led to the near breakdown of urban life . . .' The crux of the book dwells on the dilemmas of the Bolshevik government in this context, and it makes an honest appraisal of the contending oppositional forces, often based on recent facts and figures released from the Kremlin archives.

Smith dwells on the nature of revolutions and their differences and the very particular aspects of the Bolshevik revolution, which aimed to bring a socialist state into being, setting a path towards a communist future. Although referring to the October Revolution as a *coup d'état,* Smith is confident that the majority of the population, the workers and peasants, welcomed the new regime. Lenin's *April Theses* was predicated on the expected socialist revolution in Western Europe, which was thought by all factions of the Bolsheviks to be essential for the survival of their own regime. The Introduction does note the immense influence of the Soviet Union on the 20th century, but not without ruminating on the moral dimension of the revolution. Pointing out obvious tensions in the results of October, the author reflects that, whatever the enlightened aims of the Bolsheviks, these could be corrupted by 'thirst for power, the enthusiasm for violence, and contempt for law and ethics'.

Russia in Revolution takes us through the various phases leading to the revolutions with the first chapter covering the period 1880 up to the revolution of 1905, the 'dress rehearsal' for 1917. The interregnum between the 1905 revolution and its suppression, and the outbreak of World War One in 1914, is seen as a period of reaction by most radical observers. Certainly, Lenin was to opine that this period had stabilised Tsarist rule and remarked: 'we of the older generation may not live to see the decisive battles of this coming revolution'. For Wayne Dowler,a mainstream academic writer, this was a period where the development of civil society, and in particular the advancement of a cohesive middle class, heralded 'co-operation and integration'. Smith doubts Dowler's assertions, and though he agrees that 'civil society was more entrenched', he is convinced that under the calm surface lay profound dissatisfaction. For the peasant the release from serfdom was replaced by economic tyranny of rent, sharecropping and work for the landlord. The *muzhiks'* subservience in terms of their personal life continued long after the abolition of serfdom. For example, permission to marry or to leave the village was at the landowner's whim. The emergent working class was approaching 20 million, according to Smith, when one counts all those involved in construction, mines, transport, with factory workers and miners numbering about 3.6 million. The working conditions of the industrial factory worker are perhaps best described in the quotation from Leon Trotsky: 'snatched from the plough and hurled into the factory furnace'.

Chapter three charts the ebbs and flows of the build-up to the Bolshevik Revolution, and the essential role of Lenin and his successful struggle to convince the party to change course with his famous *April Theses*. The actual seizure of power is covered in a mere four pages, but recognises the indispensable role that Lenin was to play, with Trotsky in charge organisationally. Even while Lenin was still in hiding, many of the Bolshevik leadership were opposed to taking power, but Lenin would not be persuaded otherwise, firing off missives to the vacillating politburo warning, 'History will not forgive us if this opportunity to take action is missed'.

The next chapters take us through the formative years of the Bolshevik state whose infancy was forged in the fratricidal horrors of the Civil War and its accompanying trauma of foreign intervention and blockade. It was not until August 1921 that major troop engagements and foreign interventionist forays ceased, with Makhno and his anarchist army driven into exile. The cost of this violent birth was killing and suffering on a vast scale. Smith gives some indication of the numbers involved: 3.3 million Russian troops in German prison camps; 2.25 million Russian troop fatalities; Russia's financial debt doubled from 1914 to 1917 to 8 million gold roubles; by 1917 something like 9 million Russians in uniform. For Civil War casualties Smith lists 4.7 million military deaths, adding together Red and White Army fatalities, whilst accurate figures for civilian deaths resulting from atrocities, famine and disease are unknown. As to the political and economic history, there are chapters on both War Communism and the New Economic Policy (NEP) and a final chapter on the development of Soviet culture, which up until the rise of the Stalinist bureaucracy was an explosive mixture of *avant garde* in all the major art forms. The rise of the bureaucracy is exemplified in a contemporaneous quotation from an I.B Krasin, a delegate to the 10th party conference to the effect that the party consisted of '10% idealists who are ready to die for the idea, and 90% hangers-on without consciences'. Smith notes that in the party purge of 1921 some 24% of the membership were 'excluded' for such behaviour as drunkenness, careerism, unreliability, and a 'dissolute way of life'!

With the country wracked by acute food shortages, the collapse of industry, and the near total destruction of the industrial base, the Bolsheviks decided that only an extreme response would combat such a terrible situation — War Communism, as described in chapter five, a policy which forced a continuation of the organisational norms of the military. Compulsion was its main instrument, combined with an appeal to socialist instincts of self-sacrifice by putting 'politics in command'. However bleak the situation seemed to be, an iron will could overcome the problem. All this had more than a smattering of 'barracks communism', as described disapprovingly by Marx. Famine again stalked the land — forcible requisitioning of grain from the peasantry divided city and country and could not last. Reluctantly, the so-called 'New Economic Policy' was introduced, restoring market economy in many areas, particularly agriculture. The leading faction within the Politburo, led by Bukharin and Stalin, maintained that the NEP would stimulate the economy and restore balance between the town and country. Stalin later abandoned his accommodation of the peasantry, replacing it with enforced collectivisation, which was carried out at terrible human cost. Bukharin's inquisitors at his show trial must have found useful his contemporaneous appeal to kulaks and 'Nepmen' to 'enrich yourselves', but his fate, whatever he said, was sealed, and he was shot in 1938.

Russia in Revolution is, in general, sympathetic to the Bolshevik cause, but this does not inhibit the author from trenchant criticism of the use of terror in the Civil War and the activities of the Cheka. Trotsky openly defended the use of terror in his book *Terrorism and Communism*. Less erudite Bolsheviks proclaimed in the columns of the paper *Krasnyi Mech* (*Red Sword*),

> 'Everything is permitted to us, because we are the first in the world to raise the sword, not in the name of enserfment and oppression but of general happiness and liberation from slavery.'

Smith includes relatively little on the clashes in the Politburo, and the Left Opposition's struggle against the direction of march of the revolution is not fully explored. Neither does the author put much emphasis on the failure of revolution in Europe, in particular Germany, which was integral to Lenin's strategy. Lenin himself had little faith in the survival of the

Russian revolution without the aid of a radical seizure of power in Germany.

Of course, any book on the Soviet Union that is even mildly sympathetic towards Bolshevik power has to contend with the accusation that Stalin's murderous repression was a continuation of the Leninist doctrine of the Party. Rest assured this argument will continue to be debated in Left and Right circles *ad infinitum*. The argument about what kind of political formation can engender the sorts of changes necessary to bring about a successful social revolution still continues to look towards the Russian experience, and this book should be welcomed for its clarity and its willingness to examine the birth pangs of this truly momentous revolution. Certainly the author, in an internet video interview, agreed with Tariq Ali, author of *The Dilemmas of Lenin* (Verso 2017), that without Lenin there would have been no Russian Bolshevik revolution. One can't help asking the question: would Lenin have proceeded with his project if he had known the cost in human life and its outcome? Ali maintains that, without October, the White generals would have been the dominant force, dispatching to the wind the gains of February.

One particular contemporaneous observer's reflections, those of Bertrand Russell, have in part certainly stood the test of time. Russell went to Soviet Russia in 1920. He met, or saw in action, all the major actors in the revolution and was to remark unambiguously about his meeting with Lenin:

'He (Lenin) is very friendly and apparently simple, entirely without a trace of *hauteur*. If one met him without knowing who he was, one would not guess that he is possessed of great power or even that he is in any way eminent. I have never met a person so destitute of self-importance.'

In a more sombre appraisal, Russell thought Lenin too dogmatic:

'I think if I had met him without knowing who he was, I should not have guessed that he was a great man; he struck me as too opinionated and narrowly orthodox. His strength comes, I imagine, from his honesty, courage unwavering faith — in the Marxian gospel, which takes the place of Christian martyrs' hopes of Paradise, except it is less egotistical.'

Russell made an appeal to the West, which fell on deaf ears:

'But it is essential to a happy issue that melodrama should no longer determine our views of the Bolsheviks: they are neither angels to be worshipped nor devils to be exterminated, but merely bold and able men attempting with great skill an almost impossible task.'

He pointedly attacked what he conceived as the dogmatism of the Bolsheviks:

'I went to Russia a socialist: but contact with those that have no doubts has intensified a thousandfold my own doubts, not as to socialism in itself, but as to the wisdom of holding a creed so firmly that for its sake men are willing to inflict widespread misery.'

But Russell knew that if he was a Russian he would be with the Bolsheviks:

'Even under present conditions in Russia, it is still possible to feel the inspiration of the essential spirit of communism, the spirit of creative hope, seeking to sweep away the incumbrances of injustice and tyranny and rapacity which obstructs the growth of the human spirit, to replace individual competition by collective action, the relation of master and slave by free co-operation.'

In a fascinating and thoughtful Conclusion, Smith tries to make the connections between the extreme violence which was endemic in the semi-feudal Tsarist society, the directed violence of Lenin's infant state, and its apotheosis in Stalin's terror. Did Stalinism see the recall of the patrimonial state, as Richard Pipes has suggested, which finds expression in Eisenstein's film, *Ivan the Terrible*? Do we see something of this in the cult of Putin? Maybe, but the author warns, quite rightly, that 'culture is contested' and we must be careful not to fall into a tunnel vision approach when thinking about Russia. We should not forget the historical harm inflicted upon Russia by the West and the twist such pressure has applied to its social and political life. *Russia in Revolution* sheds light on the ambitions and mistakes of that tenuous first workers' state. It was driven by the finest of ambitions, as Russell saw all those years ago.

John Daniels

Savage land of Muscovy

David Burke, *Russia and the British Left: From the 1848 Revolutions to the General Strike*, I.B. Tauris, 2018, 322 pages, hardback ISBN 9781788310642, £72.00

Theodore and Andrew Rothstein dominate the narrative. With David Burke there's some sense of 'Déjà Lu all over again' (Yogi Berra). First, there was his 1997 doctoral thesis, covering the same ground, albeit stopping at 1920 (details online). Then an essay, ' Theodore Rothstein, Russian Emigré and British Socialist,' reproduced online from John Slattery's (ed.) *From the Other Shore: Russian Political Emigrants in Britain, 1880-1917*. Ancillary subsuming volumes include *The Lawn Road Flats* and *The Spy Who Came In From The Co-op* (Melita Norwood).

Though lavishly quoting from Rothstein''s multifarious articles and speeches, virtually none appear in Burke's bibliography. The online Marxist Archive provides a long list of essays in such journals as *The Communist International, The Social Democrat, Justice*, and *The Call*.

As Marx and Engels, also Lenin (Trotsky and Stalin to lesser degree), Rothstein was devoted to classical literature, writing articles on Roman poets and poetry: a shame his projected book on Cicero never materialized.

Were it not for their other manifest ineptitudes, I'd share Burke's bewilderment at British Intelligence Services' (on which he has much of interest to say) recruitment of Rothstein as an agent.

After a brief Introduction setting out his bibliographical and thematic stall, Burke opens with the careers and ideologies of Alexander Herzen and Sergei Stepnyak, nowadays hardly household names. No mention of Tom Stoppard's dramatic resuscitation of Herzen (with Bakunin, Belinsky, and Turgenev) in his 2002 trilogy *The Coast of Utopia*, his laudations (likewise Isaiah Berlin in *The Russian Thinkers*) inspired by the spectacular party Herzen threw (10 April 1861) at Ossett House (Paddington) to celebrate Tsar Alexander II's Emancipation of the Serfs.

Though anathema to Marx, Herzen remains a memorable orator-writer, abounding in aphorisms (see the website collection) such as:
'In general modern man has no solutions.'
'Human Development is a form of chronological unfairness.'
'Life has taught me to think, but thinking has not taught me to live.'
Herzen is often dubbed 'The Father of Russian Socialism'. Stepnyak, by contrast, is best remembered for assassinating secret police chief Nikolai

Mezentsov in St. Petersburg (1878), plus his own demise, hit by a train in Chiswick. For more, see David Saunder's *Oxford Dictionary of National Biography* entry, plus James Coll, *The Anarchists* (p.103) and Alex Butterworth's *The World that Never Was: A True Story of Dreamers, Schemers, Anarchists & Secret Police* (p.92) — neither in Burke.

Early in Burke's parade comes Theodore Rothstein's political mentor Wilfrid Scawen Blunt, kinsman and inspiration of Anthony. Other such past-present links include Kerensky's secretary David Soskice, father of Labour Home Secretary (under Wilson) Frank, and Donald Maclean, progenitor of the future Cambridge spy.

Also (alas), two very-modern-sounding themes pervade the book: perpetual sectarian in-fighting (Stepnyak and Plekhanov being early maddened by this permanent impediment to progress, Henry Hyndman singled out as main culprit) and rampant anti-Semitism in Labour circles, balanced by Churchill's offensive attempt to (Burke's words) engineer a split between East End and West End Jewry.

The many modern despisers of the *Daily Mail* won't be surprised by its frequent reactionary role in these early days, above all gleeful publication of the ' Zinoviev Letter', widely dismissed as a fake. At (Burke might have added) Robin Cook's behest, expert Gill Bennett's report concluded it was probably concocted by White Russians at Riga — has anyone suggested the *Mail*'s editorial office?

There's another, lighter past-present link. We all know about the Blair-Brown 'Granita' restaurant pact. A clandestine meeting between Rothstein, Litvinov and British counterparts to cement recognition of Bolshevism was held at a Lyons Corner House. When Rothstein introduced *Daily Herald* editor Meynell to potential Russian financers, it was at the luxurious Floral Frascati's restaurant — quite a step up from Joe Lyons…

Chapter 2 (Its title, 'East End Jewish Marxist', recalls Arnold Wesker's famous dramatic trilogy) concentrates on Rothstein *père* and his constant warfare with Hyndman, both foreign policy (Boer War and Persia), more importantly (and enduring — Lenin frequently adverted to it) over the relative importance of Socialist propagandizing and trade union activism. The latter can of course take embarrassing turns, e.g. Sid Harroway's 'The Social Contract? You Can Stuff It!' and London Dockers marching for Enoch. Nor would Rothstein's paraded contempt for Keir Hardy have gone down well in some circles.

These themes occupy the next chapter on London Congresses and the Second International. There is much on Wilfrid Blunt and Egyptian matters bulk large, on which Burke might have profited from Gabriel Warburg's *A History of the Egyptian Intelligence Service*, also Michael Pearce's delightful *Mamur Zapt* fictional series. Lenin appears on the London stage, so visibly that it is hard to see how British Intelligence could (p. 127) regard him as 'a mystery man'.

Lenin in London is balanced by Trotsky with his *Nashe Slovo* magazine in Paris. Their clash over 'Revolutionary Defeatism' (Lenin) and the influential Zimmerwald Manifesto (Trotsky) also figures.

In contrast with his attention to Lenin's writings, especially '*Left Wing' Communism: An Infantile Disorder,* Burke is sparing with Trotsky's. Given its timing and relevance to his own book, I'm surprised he didn't spend some time on *Where Is Britain Going?* (1925).

Another key Russian on the British scene was Georgii Chicherin, future Soviet Foreign Affairs Commissar. *Spokesman* readers will light upon one of his trade union fellow-activists — Bertrand Russell. Not that this saved the latter from a vicious personal attack by Karl Radek in *Pravda* (October 24, 1920, English version online, along with the gloss that Russell would prefer prison to giving up his sense of humour – see below).

Similarly, they will be struck by Maxim Litvinov's ill-concealed call for a British workers' armed insurrection delivered to great applause at the Labour Party Conference (1916) in Nottingham.

Space precludes the detailed attention Burke's other chapters deserve. Many, of course, are familiar: The Great War, The Bolshevik Revolution, The General Strike, all involving countless now largely forgotten participants and manoeuvres, ably disentangled by Burke.

One topic to which Burke gives oddly short thrift is the founding of the Communist Party of Great Britain (CPGB). There are, obviously, many separate accounts of this, from which I single out Francis Beckett's, if only for its title *Enemy Within*, unmentioned by Burke who does though echo the phrase, one notoriously applied to the striking coal miners by Mrs Thatcher, also adopted as their name by an American heavy metal band.

Burke sums up his main themes in a brief but illuminating Epilogue, with acute discussion of the so-called 'Henry Telling Conundrum'. His engrossing work is lucidly written, sometimes witty, jargon-free; one minor black mark for frequently repeating lengthy source quotations. It is meticulously researched from vast archival sources, conversations with Andrew Rothstein, and a plethora of articles and books, also unpublished theses. I'd have added Eric Hobsbawm's *How to Change the World: Marx and Marxism 1840-2011*. All buttressed by nearly 50 pages of tersely informative, sometimes provocative endnotes. Seventeen black-and-white plates include the first likeness of Lenin published in Britain.

Indispensable for future researchers, this admirable investigation favourably reverses the meaning of 'To Burke the issue'.

Barry Baldwin

Bertrand Russell's Sentimental Journey

Karl Radek circa 1930

Many of our British guests have published articles and books of impressions on their journey to the savage land of Muscovy. As might have been expected, true Radicals express deep sympathy for our labours and struggles, while disguised Conservatives try to help the forces which would crush us. We anticipated nothing else.

When Tom Shaw, the well-known British opportunist, asked our Soviet representatives with childlike naïveté how they could imagine that such a high-born gentleman as the Right Honourable Winston Leonard Spencer Churchill, the grandson of the Seventh Duke of Marlborough, the son of Lord Randolph Churchill, could lie, it showed that Mr. Shaw himself, although of low birth and a servant of the British bourgeoisie, would lie to injure soviet Russia at the bidding of that bourgeoisie. Consequently we were not surprised when Tom Shaw delivered a thunderous speech against the soviet government at the congress of the Yellow International, accusing it of oppressing the workmen.

The secretary of the delegation, Dr. Guest, by publishing in that yellowest of international papers, the London *Times*, a series of attacks on soviet Russia, merely proves what we were warned against when we permitted him to enter Russia, that he came to get information for the British government. In order to enable honest labour representatives to come to Russia, we had to admit also ordinary spies, who now shamelessly unmask themselves. Their 'revelations' of soviet Russia do no real harm, because every honest British workman knows, from his daily reading, that *The Times* and the whole Northcliffe press are fighting the British proletariat. He knows, too, that Dr. Guest's 'revelations,' are worth to the bourgeoisie the price he is paid for his lies. By comparing Dr. Guest's articles with those of Paul Duke, an acknowledged spy of the British government, published in the same 'honest' newspaper, any British workman can see how monotonously alike they are.

If Mrs. Ethel Snowden, the erstwhile beautiful pacifist and representative of British workmen, thought she could fascinate us by her pretty manners, it does not follow that we supposed for one minute that this bourgeois goose was competent to understand the revolution of the Russian proletariat. Being 'gallant,' we pretended to believe her enthusiasm was sincere when she told us, while watching a military review, that she quite approved of such militarism, since it was to defend the labour commonwealth. But we knew that stern proletarian revolution was not suited for Mrs. Snowden's delicate nerves, and that on her return to England, she would burst into tears upon the manly breast of Mr. Philip Snowden, who would say to her: 'Why did you go to that barbarous country? Didn't I tell you that it's not the place for British ladies to take a vacation? Better go to Belgium or to Northern France, where you can rest and visit war ruins.'

It is not worth while to discuss in detail articles written by Shaw, Guest, or Mrs. Snowden. But it is interesting to pause a moment over the two articles by Bertrand Russell in *The Nation*, the leading organ of the British liberals. Bertrand Russell is a remarkable philosopher and mathematician, as well as an absolutely honest man. He suffered persecution in a British prison for his pacifism. We believe he has no selfish purpose in writing what he does. His articles have value as demonstrating the narrowness of even the best of the bourgeoisie, their utter inability to comprehend the problems which history has placed before mankind.

Mr. Russell describes soviet Russia, stating clearly that the soviet government placed no obstacles in the way of his companions or himself and gave them full opportunity for an objective study of the Russian situation. What did he see in Russia? Of the Communists, he speaks very favourably. He says that they do not spare themselves, just as they do not spare others; that they work sixteen hours a day, forgetting about holidays; that, in spite of the power they hold, they live very modestly, seek no personal aims, but devote themselves unsparingly to building a new society. And he comes to the conclusion that the Russian. Communists are very much like the English Puritans of Cromwell's time. But

'life in Russia today, just as it was in the Puritan England, runs counter to human instinct. If the Bolsheviki fall, it will be for precisely the same reason that English Puritanism fell: time will come when people will realize that the joy of life is of greater value than anything that Puritanism has to offer.'

There is no doubt that Mr. Russell is an 'altruist'; his whole life is a proof of this. Yet Mr. Russell has not given up his comfortable home, his quiet study, his weekends in the country, his visits to the theatres, and all the other things which even the perishing capitalistic world still has to offer a man of wealth like himself.

Therefore it is no wonder that he considers a revolution in which the telephone, a piece of white bread, a can of condensed mills, or - oh, horror! - an automobile, is a luxury, is not good; for Bertrand Russell can endure such a revolution no longer than two weeks, and even then when provided by us with guest quarters and other special comforts. Therefore Mr. Russell does not ask himself what comforts would have been provided for the Russian workmen, if Kolchak, Denikin, Yudenich, and Wrangel had won a victory with British aid.

Mr. Russell considers the Communists the young, virile aristocracy of new Russia. And he says that in many respects soviet Russia reminds him of Plato's Republic. Since up to now, the word 'Plato' has not been considered derogatory, we ought to be grateful to Russell even for that. But what is hidden behind Russell's views on the situation in Russia is concretely expressed in the following words:

'When a Russian Communist speaks of dictatorship, he uses that word in a literal sense, but when he speaks of proletariat, he uses that word in a Pickwickian sense. He has in mind the class-conscious part of the proletariat, that is, the Communist Party. He includes men who have nothing in common with the proletariat so far as their origin is concerned - like Lenin and Chicherin - but who have the proper views. He excludes real workmen who do not have these views, and whom he calls lackeys of the bourgeoisie.'

What a dreadful thing, indeed, is this, which Bertrand Russell has discovered in soviet Russia! But to help him understand what he saw, let us remind him of social relations in England herself. He comes from the high aristocracy and belongs to the bourgeoisie. But when, during the war, he, as a pacifist, did not act as the bourgeoisie demanded, the latter ceased to consider him a member of the same class as itself, but threw him into prison as an enemy of that class. At the same time, it made Mr. Henderson, who is a common workman, a cabinet minister, because he defended its interests. Or let us recall a still more striking instance. One of the leaders of the Chartist movement in England was Ernest Jones, a scion of an aristocratic family. He was a godson of the Hanoverian King, and was brought up at the royal court. But when in 1846, he took part in the revolutionary agitation of the British workmen, he was thrown into prison, where he was kept for two years, under conditions which caused the death of many who were incarcerated with him.

So it appears that the unheard-of thing which Mr. Russell saw in Russia, that everyone who fights for the proletariat is a soldier of the proletariat, is something common to all struggling classes. They consider as their own those who actually fight for their interests, and not those who happen to spring from their loins.

Mr. Russell declares that he opposes communism for the same reasons for which he is a pacifist. Civil war, like any other kind of war, brings with it enormous sufferings and misfortunes, while its good is more than problematic. And in the struggle, civilization itself is doomed to perish. We have already seen how highly Mr. Russell values the civilization that has given rise to a four-year war!

To conquer, we must have a concentration of power, and every concentration of power begets evils. Mr. Russell has before him two types of the concentration of power. The first is the capitalistic government of Great Britain and its Allies, which precipitated the world into mutual slaughter, and which still ruins its happiness and welfare. Mr. Russell does not like Lloyd George; still less does he like Churchill. The second is the government of soviet Russia, which bends every effort toward rescuing the common people from the misfortunes brought upon them by capitalism. It is a government making an heroic attempt to reconstruct society from the foundation. But it cannot fight the whole capitalistic world successfully by mere guerrilla warfare. It is forced to organize a Red army, a huge food-supply apparatus, centralized economic control. But Mr. Russell says that this is not good, since it creates privilege: no matter how modest the commissars may be, still they have automobiles, the use of telephones, theatre tickets.

Now, what is Mr. Russell to do, wedged in between these two horrid governments, trying the best they can to monopolize power? Having returned from his sentimental journey, and taken a good bath, he, no doubt, seated himself in front of a fireplace - how wonderful are the old English fireplaces! Although he is not a commissar, there is no doubt that he does not have to suffer for lack of wood, even though the poor in the East End freeze to death. So, Mr. Russell put on his house slippers and dressing robe, and began to read in the newspapers of Europe's agony, which went on uninterrupted during his absence. Even Miss Gibbs writes openly about the matter in Lloyd George's own *Daily Chronicle*. As he read, there rose in Mr. Russell's heart a feeling of displeasure; for how can a good, clever, wealthy man experience pleasure, when he sees others suffering? And Mr. Russell declared in *The Nation*:

> 'Though I cannot preach the world revolution, neither can I rid myself of the conviction that the governments of the leading countries are doing everything in their power to bring it about.'

How bad are the capitalistic governments, and how good is Bertrand Russell! It is not improbable that he may again find himself in prison; and we only hope that, because of his excellent family connections, his punishment may not be excessively severe. We wish him nothing but good; but what value is there to his senseless sacrifices?

During his stay in Moscow, Bertrand Russell declared that he would rather go to prison than give up his sense of humour. We sometimes fancy that all his philosophy, all his pacifism and Socialism, are merely a way in which this scion of British aristocracy jokes at its crude oppression and maraudery. If they had only arranged things better, 'more delicately,' so that Mr. Russell could enjoy the privileges of his position without experiencing the pangs of conscience: they are so unpleasant, those pangs of conscience!

What a sorry sight does the capitalistic world present, if in the face of the most gigantic catastrophe of all history, it can devise no better philosophy than that of Mr. Russell! His philosophy reminds us of Aesop's fable of the ass, which had placed before it oats and hay, and died of starvation while debating which it should eat first. We apologize to Bertrand Russell for comparing him to so stupid a beast as an ass, but we also apologize to that honest grey toiler, for comparing him to so parasitical a being as our petty-bourgeois 'philosopher.'

Karl Radek

First Published: Pravda, October 24, 1920, *The Living Age*, January-March, 1920.
Transcription/Markup: Brian Reid **Public Domain:** Soviet History Archive 2005

How fascists organise?

Simon Winlow, Steve Hall and James Treadwell, *The rise of the Right: English nationalism and the transformation of working class politics,* **Policy Press, 2017, 219 pages, paperback SBN 99781447328483**

With the news in September 2017 that National Action, Britain's first proscribed neo-Nazi group since the 1939-45 War, had infiltrated the Army, it might be hoped that *The rise of the Right* would be able to offer important insights into how today's fascists organise and the extent of their influence. The English Defence League (EDL), ostensibly the subject of this book, appears to be different from the smaller, youth-oriented National Action, but both use violent demonstrations to incite racial hatred (the EDL specifically anti-Muslim feeling) and both actively use social media to spread their views and to organise demonstrations. They are both opportunist: the EDL blatantly targeting towns and cities such as Rotherham to foment anti-Muslim feeling, while National Action have been behind offensive publicity stunts (such as organising a Hitler salute outside York Minster) to promote white supremacist ideas.

The authors (all white, male British professors) interviewed EDL activists and fellow-travellers to enable the reader 'however briefly, to see the world as EDL supporters see it'. They acknowledge that some will say this gives the EDL 'publicity' and 'credibility' but, in their view:

'...those who simply oppose what they do not understand are running away from the political reality of our times. If social scientists are to assist in the task of making sense of that reality, we can't simply restrict ourselves to the nice topics. We can't simply praise the nice people and condemn the bad...'

This is both simplistic and patronising. They then comment that their analysis of the wider context which spawned the EDL may not be welcomed by many on what they call the 'political and academic left' who might:

'... feel uncomfortable and perhaps mildly aggrieved. No matter. We will report the world as we found it, and we will explain that world in a manner that seems to us useful and appropriate.'

So just having turned a few pages, we wondered if reviewing this book was a good idea. Nevertheless, it was read from cover to cover including the authors' blog from the Policy Press website, which is included at the end of the book. This was written after the EU referendum in June 2016, and has an air of 'we *told you so*' in relation to the way immigration rather than the economy affected the way the referendum vote divided in many places.

So how useful is this book? Generally, there is a problem with the tone, especially in the early chapters 'Dead politics' and 'The fickle parent'. For example, there is anger, contempt and name-calling in their account of the politics of New Labour and the Coalition Government, and it is often difficult to disentangle their opinions from what is factually based as there are few references to authoritative work. For example, their account of times before and after the 2008 financial crisis is too sweeping. It is not sufficiently focused on austerity measures that have had a devastating effect on working-class individuals, families and communities. This is important because many of the EDL members they spoke to claimed that the recent decline of their community was what propelled them into action: drugs, deteriorating services and shops and, in some places, a Muslim presence which they did not want. It would have helped to have placed these comments in their appropriate contexts. To what extent was the EDL response typical? Without this, and a more cautious evaluation of what the authors were being told, it often seemed as if the authors considered the EDL and the 'white working class' as synonymous, which is far from the case.

The next four chapters concentrate on the comments and conversations the authors had with EDL members up to 2015 in their homes, down the pub, on street corners and at the bookies. There are four 'themes', indicated by the chapter headings: 'Redundant,' 'The hated centre,' 'The scapegoat' and 'Mourning and melancholia'. In each chapter, the format is introductory remarks followed by long quotations from individual interviews/conversations and then an analytical section followed by a conclusion. In 'The scapegoat' EDL members explain why they hate Muslim families and Islam. In 'The hated centre" their abhorrence of politicians, especially Labour Party and left-leaning politicians, is detailed (what the authors confusingly often berate as the 'metropolitan liberal elite').

The comments in these chapters are often outrageous, but familiar: EDL members denying they are racist or fascist and that all they want to do is alert the general public to the apparent dangers of Muslim culture and Islam. The authors make the point that EDL supporters, apart from the 'hard-liners,' seem to have a limited involvement span. The organisation does not appear to have a leadership or 'vanguard,' is not interested in parliamentary politics, and is unable to move on from violent street protest. But the authors' treatment of EDL members' comments seems to be incomplete and naive in places. For example, for supporters attending a demonstration, being corralled into side streets by police and shouted at by anti-fascists may be exciting to begin with:

'Many of our contacts who were active in street protests were or had been involved in football hooliganism. Heading to a street protest in another town or city was just like going to an away game, and for a time, that's what they liked about it. They would start drinking early on, maybe have a few lines of cocaine and a bit of a laugh with the lads, then they would experience the adrenaline of spilling off the coach to be surrounded by opponents and quite often the police. There was also a chance they might get to throw a few punches, and return home with a story to tell.'

But it wore a bit thin for them after a while, with a larger and more controlling police presence and more effective anti-fascist counter-demonstrations and publicity. If these professors had possessed wider experience and knowledge, they would have linked football hooliganism in the EDL to similar links within their predecessors, the British National Party, the National Front, the British Movement, the League of Empire Loyalists and the British Union of Fascists. Instead, they claim that ultimately they came to the conclusion that the EDL could not move on because it 'couldn't find a leader or a political ideology because it was a reluctant and fragile entity forged purely on postmodern cynicism and negativity'. Really?

The way in which EDL supporters are treated in this book should raise alarm bells. When does it become unacceptable to reproduce long, offensive and intimidating fascist rants? While the comments of EDL supporters (who were usually men) were not always taken at face value, most of them must have avoided talking about their use of intimidating and violent behaviour at demonstrations. Why was there no evaluation of the impact of these on particular local areas? And why was the content of EDL websites and use of social media not the subject of detailed scrutiny? By omitting these, the authors were susceptible to being deliberately misled by part-truths. Worse still, the reader might be left under-estimating the continuing impact of the EDL's anti-Muslim rhetoric.

Cathy Davis and Alan Wigfield

From December 2016, support or membership of National Action, an anti-Semitic, white supremacist group became a criminal offence under the 2000 Terrorism Act. The Anti-Fascist Network and the Centre for Fascist, Anti-Fascist and Post-Fascist Studies at Teeside University can provide more information.

THE
DOOMSDAY
MACHINE

CONFESSIONS OF A
NUCLEAR WAR
PLANNER

DANIEL
ELLSBERG

Bloomsbury

Scorching

Daniel Ellsberg, *The Doomsday Machine: Confessions of a nuclear war planner*, Bloomsbury, 2017, 432 pages, hardback ISBN 9781408889299, £20

It's not every day that an insider tells us how preparations for nuclear war have been proceeding. So, when one does, it's worth sitting up and taking notice.

Although Daniel Ellsberg is best known for his 1971 role in delivering the Pentagon Papers (the top secret Defense Department study of US involvement in Vietnam) to the American people, he spent much of his 13-year career as a military analyst at the highest levels of the US national security apparatus grappling with issues of nuclear war.

Ellsberg's tasks for the Rand Corporation and the Defense Department included studying how to deter, avert, control, limit, or terminate a nuclear Armageddon between the United States and the Soviet Union, providing McGeorge Bundy (President Kennedy's national security advisor) with an early briefing on existing nuclear planning, and writing the Kennedy administration's top secret guidance for the US operational plan for general nuclear war. In addition, he was the only person to serve on two of the working groups reporting to the executive committee of the US National Security Council during the Cuban Missile Crisis. In 1963, he was the sole researcher in a government study of past US nuclear crises, with a classified access several levels above 'top secret'. As he writes here:

'These functions gave me an unusual knowledge . . . of the nature of the plans and operations of the nuclear forces and the dangers these posed.'

This background informed Ellsberg's decision to copy and release much more than the Pentagon Papers. Horrified by what he had learned about the readiness of the United States and the Soviet Union to exterminate a substantial portion of the human race, he copied everything in his government files with the intention of exposing it to public scrutiny and discussion. He released the Vietnam material first, for war was already ravaging that land. But he always regarded his nuclear records as more important, for they revealed how fragile the survival of world civilization had become. Ironically, however, the nuclear material, hidden by Ellsberg's brother in a compost pile and, later, in the hillside adjoining a garbage dump, was buried or swept away in a tropical hurricane.

Consequently, bringing the full range of his nuclear revelations to public attention took Ellsberg considerably longer than he anticipated. Over the following decades, while giving lectures and participating in numerous antinuclear conferences and demonstrations, he laboriously reconstructed his missing files from memory, located documents through Freedom of Information Act requests, and drew upon newly declassified government records. He also spoke with national security officials and read extensively on nuclear issues. Nevertheless, despite Ellsberg's extraordinary knowledge of nuclear war planning and the overriding importance of confronting the issue of human survival in the nuclear age, 17 publishers rejected *The Doomsday Machine* before it was finally accepted for publication. The result, though, is a book commensurate with Ellsberg's courage and unwavering determination — eloquent, honest, and packed with fascinating revelations.

Perhaps the most startling of the revelations is that the leaders of the nuclear powers have delegated authority to initiate nuclear war to military commanders and even to their military subordinates. After Ellsberg discovered the adoption of this alarming policy by the Eisenhower Administration, he reported it to the Kennedy White House, only to find that Kennedy continued it, as did Presidents Johnson, Nixon, Carter, and— as he notes— 'almost certainly . . . every subsequent president to this day'. Indeed, General Curtis LeMay, the US Air Force Chief of Staff, argued that, when it came to launching a nuclear war, US presidents should be left out of the picture entirely. 'After all,' LeMay remarked gruffly to Ellsberg and a White House official, 'who is more qualified to make that decision: some politician . . . or a man who has been preparing all his adult life to make it?' According to Ellsberg, 'it is virtually certain' that this same secret delegation of authority to military officers 'exists in every nuclear state'.

The reason for the remarkable looseness of command in launching a nuclear holocaust is that the leaders of nuclear-armed nations fear a 'decapitating' nuclear strike that, by snuffing out their centralized command and control systems, will prevent them from ordering a retaliatory nuclear assault. Therefore, they gravitate towards diversifying their opportunities for waging nuclear war. In the Soviet Union and, later, Russia, the authorities went so far as to establish a 'Dead Hand' system in which machines have the authority to launch a full-scale nuclear war in response to an American attack on their central command and control system.

Ellsberg's discussion of the reasons for the development and maintenance of the massive US nuclear weapons system is less startling, though no less disturbing. 'The *declared* official rationale for such a system,' he observes, 'has always been primarily the supposed need to deter— or if necessary respond to —an aggressive Russian nuclear first strike against the United States'. But that's 'a deliberate deception,' he contends, for that 'has *never* been . . . the primary purpose of our nuclear plans and preparations'. Instead, they represent an 'attempt to limit the damage to the United States from Soviet or Russian retaliation to a *U.S. first strike* against the USSR or Russia'. In particular, this nuclear capability is 'intended to strengthen the credibility of US threats to initiate limited nuclear attacks, or escalate them . . . to prevail in regional, initially non-nuclear conflicts'.

Ellsberg reports that,

'contrary to the cliché that "no nuclear weapons have been used since Hiroshima and Nagasaki," US presidents *have used* our nuclear weapons dozens of times in "crises," mostly in secret from the American public (though not from adversaries).'

US officials have employed them as threats, just as 'a gun is used when it is pointed at someone in a confrontation'— to 'get one's way'. Thus, for example, the Nixon Administration threatened the government of North Vietnam with a nuclear attack on 13 occasions. Ellsberg also outlines 24 other US government threats, from Presidents Truman through Clinton, to initiate nuclear war against a variety of countries.

Naturally, to bolster these threats, the US government has insisted upon not only the massive nuclear arsenal needed for a 'first strike' (a nuclear attack on an enemy's nuclear facilities to prevent retaliation), but the right to 'first use' of nuclear weapons (the initiation of nuclear war). Ellsberg notes that no major party presidential candidate or president 'has ever come close to adopting and proclaiming a no-first-use policy'. Asked about a nuclear attack upon Iran in 2006, President George W. Bush stated emphatically: 'all options are on the table.' During the 2007-2008 Democratic presidential primary campaign, Barack Obama temporarily went off message and, asked by a reporter whether there was any circumstance in which he'd use nuclear weapons in Afghanistan or Pakistan to defeat al-Qaeda, replied: 'that's not on the table'. Naturally, his rival, Hillary Clinton, seized on this brief departure from the holy writ of US national security policy to chide him, remarking: 'I don't believe any president should make any blanket statements with respect to the use or non-use of nuclear weapons'. Similarly, during the 2016 presidential campaign, Donald Trump, pressed by an interviewer about his willingness to launch a US nuclear attack in the Middle East, declared that he 'would never take any of my cards off the table'.

One of the most chilling aspects of this book is Ellsberg's revelation of how close the world has been —and remains —to nuclear annihilation. Nuclear war, he argues, is 'a catastrophe waiting to happen', and he provides many examples of how nations have been sliding toward it thanks to the growing acceptability of targeting civilian populations, the delegation of launching authority to military officers, the ruthlessness of military officers and other national security officials, false alarms, and unexpected events. During the 1962 Cuban Missile Crisis, he remarks, the United States and the Soviet Union came within 'a hairsbreadth' of ending world civilization, despite the fact that Khrushchev and Kennedy 'were determined to avoid armed conflict'.

How did this paradoxical situation develop? As Ellsberg explains, the risk of a nuclear war between the superpowers grew exponentially during the Missile Crisis thanks to the fact that a Soviet missile crew, acting on its own authority, destroyed a US U-2 flight over Cuba and that Castro's armed forces, already firing on low-flying US reconnaissance planes, were getting closer to hitting them. Also, although the US government didn't know it, there were 42,000 Soviet troops in Cuba, armed (among other things) with over 100 tactical nuclear weapons, and the Soviet government had agreed to delegate authority to local military commanders to use them to repel a US invasion. The situation was clearly spinning out of control. Khrushchev later recalled: 'a smell of scorching hung in the air'.

Meanwhile, US warships cornered a Soviet submarine in the Caribbean and attempted to force it to surface by bombarding it with depth charges. The submarine's top officers, considering themselves under attack, were cut off from outside communications and unsure whether a US-Soviet war had already begun. Moreover, the submarine's ventilator system had broken down, temperatures in the vessel ranged from 113 to 140 degrees Fahrenheit, and crew began collapsing from the extreme heat and carbon dioxide build-up. Increasingly desperate, the Soviet officers wondered whether they should fight back by firing their nuclear torpedo at the US warships. After a four-hour assault on the submarine — which one Soviet officer later said 'felt like you were sitting in a metal barrel, which somebody is blasting with a sledgehammer' — the exhausted Soviet submarine commander 'became furious' and ordered the nuclear torpedo readied for battle. Justifying the order, another emotional officer cried out:

'We're going to blast them now! We will die, but we will sink them all — we will not disgrace our Navy!' But, as another officer recalled, the submarine's commander 'was able to rein in his wrath' and, after consultation with top officers on board, made the decision to bring the vessel peacefully to the surface. As a result, an almost certain escalation into a full-scale nuclear war was averted — but only narrowly.

And what would the results of a full-scale nuclear war have been at that time? In 1961, Ellsberg discovered that the US Joint Chiefs of Staff estimated that 600 million Russians and Chinese would die from a US first strike. In addition, another 100 million or so would die in the East European satellite countries, plus (thanks to the radioactive fallout) up to another 100 million people in the surrounding neutral countries and up to another 100 million in America's West European NATO allies. Also, of course, there would be a great many millions of additional people killed by the Soviet Union's nuclear response. Furthermore, as Ellsberg notes, this was a 'fantastic underestimate', for it was based on fatalities from nuclear blast and fall-out, and did not include deaths by fire.

Today, of course, the destruction from a full-scale nuclear war would be far greater. The shift in nuclear arsenals from atomic bombs to Hydrogen (H) Bombs (weapons that can be made a thousand times as powerful as the bomb that destroyed Hiroshima) has certainly upped the ante. Moreover scientists have discovered and confirmed the phenomenon of "nuclear winter," in which the soot and smoke from a large number of nuclear explosions would be lofted into the upper stratosphere. This, in turn, would create global darkness and cold that would destroy the world's agriculture, thereby leading to massive starvation and the death of nearly every human left alive on earth, along with that of most other large species.

Ellsberg's conclusion is stark, but follows logically from this evidence
.

'Any social system', he writes, 'that has created and maintained a Doomsday Machine and has put a trigger to it, including first use of nuclear weapons, in the hands of one human being —. . . still worse in the hands of an unknown number of persons — is in core aspects mad. Ours is such a system. Wc are in the grip of institutionalized madness.'

Although Ellsberg is pessimistic about the prospects of human survival, he is not without remnants of hope or recommendations for action. 'The US government,' he writes, 'pressed by a popular movement and preferably backed by binding congressional legislation', should proclaim 'that there is no "nuclear first-use option" on the bargaining table in our dealings with

. . . any nation.' Indeed, first use of nuclear weapons is 'not a legitimate "option" for the United States, Russia, or for any other country under any circumstances.' Other 'necessary goals' include reducing the role of the world's nuclear weapons to deterrence while securing, as rapidly as possible, the 'total universal abolition of nuclear weapons'.

Ellsberg's top priority, though, is the dismantling of the Doomsday Machines of the United States and Russia through drastic reductions in their nuclear arsenals. As he reminds us:

> 'No cause, no principle, no considerations of honour or obligation or prestige or maintaining leadership in current alliances — still less, no concern for remaining in office or maintaining a particular power structure, or sustaining jobs, profits, votes — can justify maintaining any risk whatever of causing the near extinction of human and other animal life on this planet.'

Omnicide— whether threatened, prepared, or carried out — 'cannot be regarded as anything less than criminal, immoral, evil'.

Whether the people of the world will take this message to heart remains uncertain. It's tempting to ignore it for, like the evidence of human-instigated climate disruption, it necessitates a significant change in behaviour. And it's sometimes easier to continue a bad habit — even when it leads to harmful consequences — than to face up to the necessity for change.

But, as Ellsberg's brilliantly written, deeply insightful, and powerful book should convince us, continued preparations for nuclear war seriously threaten the survival of most life on earth. Also, in fact, millions of people in nations around the globe have already spoken out against government plans for nuclear annihilation, demanding, instead, nuclear disarmament. Perhaps, ultimately, humanity will have the wisdom and strength to prevail.

Lawrence S. Wittner

www.lawrencewittner.com
Professor of history emeritus at SUNY/Albany
and author of Confronting the Bomb *(Stanford University Press)*

Cordiality and cunning

Chico Buarque translated by Alison Entrekin, *My German Brother*, Picador, 2018, 200 pages, hardback ISBN 9781509806454, £14.99

Chico Buarque is, above all, a realist and a pragmatist, a master of genres who is at the same time chary of classification. Social responsibility or activism in Brazil, of the kinds engaged in by Chico the singer-songwriter during the military dictatorship (1964-1980) or, more recently, in support of the deposed Lula and the *Partido dos Trabalalhadores*, are far from the aspirations of any of his fictional protagonists. They are, rather, *malandros,* or practitioners of *jeitinho,* who apply a local cunning to the exigencies of day to day survival, scrabbling for a foothold in the conflicted urban terrain of Rio or Sao Paulo. Chico's anthems have always reverberated at the barricades, in the stadia or during Carnival, providing a camaraderie they acknowledge as temporary like that of '*A Banda',* in which, after the samba has passed through the neighbourhood, 'each one [is again] in his corner / in every corner its pain'. They are also part, whether they like it or not, of what Luiz Eduardo Soares, Lula's one time National Secretary for Public Security, decries as the delusory, hedonistic façade of the Brazilian 'Extreme City' [Penguin, 2016] with its hollow claims to 'racial democracy', behind which nightmarish poverty and brutality sprawl.

'I didn't need to visit a favela to write about its people', Chico told the *Financial Times* in 2004: perhaps it's enough that his songs travel there, one commentator glossing this kind of disingenuousness as a 'complex stance toward Brazil's poor, which oscillates between empathetic identification and an almost arch sense of ironic distance' [Caio Camargo]. But in each of the (so far) five novels, however much the displaced *malandros* writhe in the toils of their own self-interest and venality – they all come from aristocratic, affluent or intellectual circles, pedigrees replete with plantation-owners, senators, cosmopolitan or corporate connections, and are as desperate to reclaim some vestige of their former privileges as a Beckettian character is to climb back into his mother's womb – the other reality lamented by Soares keeps breaking through. It may take the form of the many 'Heart of Darkness' moments, ghostly incarnations of collective suffering picked up on the narrator's blunted radar which almost, but never quite, trigger a human response, like the misery of the crop gatherers employed by a local drug lord in *Turbulence*: 'At dusk they limp up the hillside, the men carrying baskets on their shoulders and the women balancing them on their heads ... I can't work out how many there are, as they're walking in groups and all look equally thin and equally flaccid'. Or of the 'profane fantasies' of the post-colonial mentality, the 100 year old bedridden son of an abolitionist yearning for the mango trees of his childhood and the freed slave climbing there in *Spilt Milk*: 'I got it into my head that I needed to take Balbino up the arse'. Solipsism stalked by atrocity — where in all this, we may ask and are, one suspects, meant to ask, is the real Chico?

My German Brother is the nearest we are likely to come, perhaps, to autobiography. Whereas *Spilt Milk* detailed the rancorous conservatism, xenophobia and arms trading of a baronial line in freefall from the mansions of Batafogo through modest apartments in Tijuca to the tender mercies of a Rio public hospital – Chico's most lurid and audacious social commentary to date – the new novel plunges us into an array of textual games that signal, like the earlier *Budapest*, the author's commitment to postmodern artifice. It's as if *My German Brother* were just one more item amid the Borgesian vastness of Sergio Buarque de Hollander's [sic] library, which incarcerates the great Brazilian sociologist and man of letters (and Chico's real father) and seals him off not only from the tumultuous history of, in this case, Sao Paulo but also of his own family. 'We remain exiles in our own land', Buarque Senior's profoundly influential study *Roots of Brazil* (1936) avowed of the Ibero-American condition in general, an observation that, additionally, might apply to intelligentsias everywhere, whether colonial, post-colonial, or indigenous: here, the lifelong pursuit of a *magnum opus* which would be 'the best book in *tutto el mondo*' is rendered as affectionate comedy but also, with withering scorn, as the cause of his fictional son Ciccio's personal anguish and lack of connection to all social developments or causes, save opportunistically. 'When no-one was around, I'd spend hours sidling along the bookcases; my back brushing from book to book gave me a certain pleasure' – the restlessness of all the *malandros* is repeated here, in the inner sanctum of childhood, as it is by the travelling finger of the mature author which, on page after page and for the duration of the novel, presents to our gaze the assembled works of world literature from *The Golden Bough* and *La Comedie Humaine* to Pasternak, *Ulysses* and W.G.Sebald (one feels in this movement the desire, still incompletely realised more than three decades later, for international recognition expressed by Garcia Marquez's Nobel Prize speech, 'The Solitude of Latin America'). Ciccio's meagre professional survival as a blogger defending his father's intellectual legacy and a 'social media-based grammar guru' only confirms the dispiriting impression of lives lived as if there were no *hors-texte.*

As the title suggests, however, the whole of *My German Brother* is premised on another order of being, and the seemingly authentic, often handwritten documents woven across its length point to an outcome whereby even tragic Ciccio, but especially Chico, can emerge again into the light of at least a limited historical reality. Chico's belated discovery that Sergio Buarque de Hollanda, wrestling with the initial stages of *The Roots of Brazil* during a prolonged stay in the Berlin of the early 1930s, sired a long lost, unidentified brother, turns what might have been just another privileged picaresque traversal of, mostly, the safer end of the Brazilian cityscape into a slow burning personal epiphany. Nor does Chico forget to remind us, *en route*, of the encircling brutalities of the dictatorship, the street killings and torture of left wing dissent or the parallels with Nazism, in images of, as always, harrowing viscerality – however fleetingly glimpsed. The library is itself subjected to violent, destructive incursions, and infested from the outset with cockroaches: 'four – lay writhing, belly-up … in the Polish gas chambers people had died gasping just like that, in the hope of finding a little oxygen above the insecticide'. But the author's playfulness, even in such circumstances, is irrepressible: a police inspector named 'Jorge Borges' flicks through a first edition of *El Aleph* with 'a stubby, dirty-nailed thumb', high and low castes parading their mutual disdain as the ransacking of the postmodern citadel proceeds. Miraculously, in the final chapter, it's Chico, not Ciccio, who steps forward *in propria persona* and out of the fictional narrative into the Berlin of 2013, the textual games cease, and the appalling modern histories of two nations drop away. In their place we seem to witness, poignantly, an enactment of the emotional 'cordiality' identified by Buarque Senior as the defining characteristic of Brazilian social behaviour, for good or ill, but here exhibited in the simple good will, compassion and practical involvement with which the citizens of the former Reich surround the author and carry him to his goal.

Stephen Winfield

The Red Decade

Richard Vinen, *The Long '68: Radical Protest and Its Enemies*, Allen Lane, 2018, 446 pages, hardback ISBN 9780241343425, £20

In 1971, Allen Lane the Penguin Press published *Prevent the Crime of Silence,* which had the lengthy sub-title, *Reports from the sessions of the International War Crimes Tribunal, founded by Bertrand Russell.* Noam Chomsky contributed a Foreword and additional chapter, 'After Pinkville', to this notable volume on Vietnam, edited by Ken Coates, Peter Limqueco and Peter Weiss. In November 1966 in London, Russell had concluded his address to the first meeting of the members of the War Crimes Tribunal with the words 'may this Tribunal prevent the crime of silence'. Jean-Paul Sartre was to preside at the two public sessions in Sweden and Denmark, alongside Vladimir Dedijer. Tribunal members included the writer James Baldwin, the lawyer Lelio Basso, and writer and philosopher Simone de Beauvoir, among activists from a number of countries.

In 1968 in the United States, O'Hare Books of New Jersey had already published *Against the Crime of Silence: Proceedings of the Russell International War Crimes Tribunal,* edited by John Duffett.

Neither Russell nor the War Crimes Tribunal figure in Richard Vinen's *The Long '68,* which has the curious sub-title *Radical protest and its enemies.* Curious because 'enemies' seems to overstate Vinen's softly spoken and generally broad-brush and wide-ranging approach to what proved to be the 'red decade', which Coates and others eagerly anticipated when they gathered as Labour Students in the late 1950s. Vinen's 'Brief Chronology' begins in April 1960 with the foundation of the Parti Socialiste Unifié in France, concluding in May 2017 with Emmanuel Macron's election as President of France, supported by Daniel Cohn-Bendit, tagged as 'Danny the Red' in the 1960s. Understandably, Vinen has a particular emphasis on the events in Paris of May and June 1968, whilst not neglecting what was happening elsewhere in France. The United States, West Germany and Britain also fall within his purview.

In his chapter entitled 'Workers', Vinen mentions that Ken Coates founded the Institute for Workers' Control in 1968. Certainly, the IWC was constituted with its council during that year, 'with the blessing of Hugh Scanlon and Jack Jones, leaders of the Engineers and Transport Workers respectively', as Ken wrote in *Workers' Control: Another world is possible* (Spokesman, 2003). But the IWC had a long prehistory, stretching back to

1963, with five national conferences bringing together shop stewards, community activists and adult educators such as Michael Barratt Brown, Ken Coates and Tony Topham. 'Most of these people came from the political left, but not all', wrote Coates, adding 'there was a strong Young Liberal input from some of the earliest conferences, and older members soon joined in'. Vinen notes Young Liberal participation.

Vinen's paragraph on Coates and the IWC is preceded by one on *autogestion*, which he translates as 'self-management'. 'The word could be applied to almost any context in which people can be seen as taking control of their own lives', comments Vinen. In the early 1950s, as a young miner, Ken Coates's own interest in self-management manifested in his support for Yugoslavia's innovations in that direction, as President Tito and Federal Yugoslavia took their distance from the Soviet Union under Stalin. This and, in 1952, the show trials and executions of Joseph Slansky and others in Czechoslovakia, thought to be sympathetic to Tito, led to Ken's departure from the Communist Party. Viner labels Ken 'Trotskyist'. Ken certainly knew all the 'groupuscules' and many of their members; the numbers were not large. However, his socialism was rooted in the quest for a wider democracy in many aspects of life, which is where he found common ground with Bertrand Russell, with whom he worked from 1965 until Russell's death in 1970. Thereafter, Ken continued his democratic quest through the IWC and the Russell Foundation, as recounted in long interviews with George Lambie prior to his death in 2010 (see *Spokesman 116*).

Tony Simpson

SECURITY *without* NUCLEAR DETERRENCE

Commander Robert Green, Royal Navy (Ret'd)

Eight years on from the first edition, worsening relations between the West and Russia, and the US and North Korea, have brought nuclear weapons back to the forefront of world attention and public concern.

Almost thirty years after the Cold War ended, some 14,500 nuclear weapons remain; and the nuclear weapon states are all modernising their nuclear arsenals. They cite nuclear deterrence doctrine as the final, indispensable justification for maintaining them. This drives the spread of nuclear weapons to paranoid regimes and extremists who are least likely to be deterred.

The fallacies of nuclear deterrence must therefore be exposed and alternatives offered if there is to be any serious prospect of eliminating nuclear weapons.

A former operator of British nuclear weapons, Commander Green has drawn together a concise, carefully researched and documented account of the history, practicalities and dangerous contradictions at the heart of nuclear deterrence. He offers more credible, effective and responsible alternative strategies to deter aggression and achieve real security.

Vice Admiral Sir Jeremy Blackham KCB, MA, a leading authority on deterrence, has written a major new Foreword to this edition, on the most sensitive and contentious issue in British defence policy with huge implications for the effectiveness, image and ethos of the Royal Navy. He concludes:

'*This is a most important contribution to the debate on a subject which is crucial to the survival of the human race, and it needs to be read with a degree of humility and an open mind – qualities not always apparent among our decision makers and their advisers.*'

Published by: Spokesman Books
Price: £14.99, Publication date: May 2018
Paperback 266 pages, with colour illustrations
ISBN 9780 85124 8721